Pittsburgh Series in Composition, Literacy, and Culture

David Bartholomae and Jean Ferguson Carr, Editors

'Round My Way

. . . .

Authority and Double-Consciousness in Three Urban High School Writers

Eli C. Goldblatt

University of Pittsburgh Press

Pittsburgh and London

ADT-9629

Published by the University of Pittsburgh Press, Pittsburgh, Pa. 15260
Eurospan, London
Manufactured in the United States of America
Printed on acid-free paper

Designed by Jane Tenenbaum

Goldblatt, Eli.
    'Round my way : authority and double-consciousness in three urban high school
writers / Eli C. Goldblatt.
      p. cm. — (Pittsburgh series in composition, literacy, and culture)
    Includes bibliographical references.
    ISBN 0-8229-3879-0 (alk. paper). — ISBN 0-8229-5563-6 (pbk. : alk. paper)
    1. Creative writing (Secondary)—Pennsylvania—Philadelphia.   2. Literature and
society—Pennsylvania—Philadelphia.   3. Diaries—Authorship.   4. High school
students—Pennsylvania—Philadelphia—Biography.   5. Education, Urban—
Pennsylvania—Philadelphia.
    6. Goldblatt, Eli.   I. Title.   II. Series.
    LB1631.G617 ~~1994~~ 1995
    808'.0071'2—dc20   95-3284
                                                 CIP

A CIP catalogue record for this book is available from the
British Library.

To the students of Neighborhood Academy
and especially to Maria, Tita, Kareem,
and their classmates

The act of being, the act of being
More than oneself.

—George Oppen

Contents

Acknowledgments

This project started as a dissertation at the University of Wisconsin-Madison in 1987. It has grown in ways I could not have predicted, but in some respects what I set out to do has not changed. I wanted to tell a human story framed by a social theory of writing, to trace the lines of power relations and political forces through the specifics of a few students' writing lives. This turned out to be a tricky undertaking both methodologically and rhetorically. I am indebted to many people for helping me push forward with my work, although none should take blame for the inevitable flaws in this particular text.

At Wisconsin, I was terribly fortunate to meet professors and students who challenged and supported me, listened enthusiastically to my ideas even when what I said must have seemed idiosyncratic at best. Martin Nystrand and Deborah Brandt were my guides and companions through the composition literature, and this book could simply not have come into being without them. Brad Hughes in the Writing Lab helped me see the theory put into practice. Cyrena Pondrom, Betsy Draine, and Lynn Keller assisted me in developing the sense of literary criticism that I brought with me to composition studies. Laurie Beth Clark, in the Art Department, nurtured my impulse toward experimentation and my interest in performance, both of which were crucial in forging the combination of research, theory, and storytelling in *'Round My Way*. I am particularly indebted to Craig Werner of the Afro-American Department for introducing me to the concept of "double-consciousness" in Du Bois and other African-American writers, and for being the colleague and friend I so needed in my last years of graduate school. Among nonfaculty friends who kept me on task with their intelligence and good humor were John Gruesser, Sylvan Esh, Mary Jo Heck, Paige Byam, Tandy Sturgeon, and John Wolff. Artist Cris Bruch and poet Chuck Alexander kept reminding me that theory, art, and analysis live under the same thatched roof.

My dedication can only indicate what I owe to the people associ-

ated with "Neighborhood Academy." I wish I could use their real
names to thank them. The director and teachers at the school were my
close associates during 1988–89, and "Anthony Marioni" taught me
more about teaching during our years together at the school than anyone in my professional life. The kids and their worlds transformed mine;
I owe them big.

In Philadelphia, many colleagues sustained my commitment to this
book and to the discipline of composition studies. Chief among them
are Karyn Hollis, Reggie Young, Evan Radcliffe, Shelley Baum-
Brunner, and Michael Smith. They each read chapters from the manuscript and gave me invaluable criticism and encouragement. In many
conversations about rhetoric and writing, Sue Wells, Frank Sullivan,
Arabella Lyon, and Tom Hemeter pressed me to see composition from
angles I did not naturally consider. John Landreau and Chris Hill and
Ellen Schelly Hill have been solid friends through it all.

Thanks, too, to David Bartholomae at the University of Pittsburgh
Press for his support throughout the process of turning the dissertation
into a book. David's belief in the project allowed me to take risks and
assume my own authority in a field where institutional identity is not
easy to represent. Composition studies arises out of a bewildering variety of disciplines, and compositionists function within many kinds of
departments, programs, and educational levels. The theory in this book
is meant to speak across these institutionalized compartments. I needed
a sponsor for this project who would not force me into a single disci-
plinary mold, and David and the press offered me such sponsorship. At
the press, also, I must thank Kathy McLaughlin for her careful and
patient editing.

Family is mentioned last here but appears everywhere in the text
and the history of composing it. My brother Aaron Goldblatt, sister-
in-law Diane Pontius, and their daughter Lilly have patiently listened
to me expatiate upon this book over many family dinners. My mother
Selma Goldblatt read drafts of many of the chapters. Her comments
have enriched this text, and her concern both for the power of words
and the need for social justice are two of the most valuable gifts she has
given me. My wife Wendy Osterweil read and commented on a number
of versions of this manuscript with an artist's eye for detail and a teacher's eye for the main point. As helpful as her criticism was, however,

her response to drafts was not her most essential contribution to the project.

The gift both Wendy and my son Leo continually give me is a life rich in shared concerns. The book always mattered but never dominated, and it took shape among diapers and toys, job hassles and child-care arrangements, art exhibits and poetry readings. We lived, and the book grew along with us. Wendy and Leo helped me see that intellectual work can thrive when it is situated in the day-to-day rather than isolated from it. To them I owe whatever is fresh and unponderous about this work.

'Round My Way

1

. . . .

Neighborhood
Academy

As any teacher who listens will know, there is a poetry to the give and take of the classroom. I do not mean that students or teachers produce pretty speech as a rule—far from it. The lectures and whispers, the questions and answers, the phrases written on the board, the notes passed hand to hand, the jotted-down, half-understood comments, the flawed and partial "assignments" turned in at the last minute or beyond, all these are the unlovely traces of a raw poetry constantly unfolding. The sentences spoken or written for classroom exchange are soaked in ambitions, fears, regrets, yearnings; they smolder, fizzle, or explode depending on the ambient temperature, oxygen content, and social pressure. The poetry of the classroom is a mélange assembled by law six hours a day from the other daily poetries of the street, the kitchen, the bedroom, the playground. Books may supply a portion of that poetry, too, but often they are merely an excuse for the mix.

This book is about the poetry and attendant stories I found in the prose and talk of three Philadelphia high school students. This is not a study of verse lines or alliteration, but an intimate and speculative look at the personae, yearnings, and contradictions their language dramatized. My project is part journalism and part literary criticism, part novel and part autobiography, part theory and part lore. Perhaps most, it is a story about my readings of the texts these students wrote in my English class. What I offer readers is not so much a "study" as a multidimensioned compendium of stories (or is it, in fact, one story?) about three young people I came to care for and respect during a single school year. I believe my focus on their writing is not just an excuse to pry. I hope it will be an opportunity to make real for a wide audience the circumstances that come to bear on certain city high school writers when they sit down to write.

There are two major threads in this book, two plot lines intertwined. The first involves school journals and papers written by Maria, Tita, and Kareem, three teenagers I taught during the 1988–89 academic year at a school I call here "Neighborhood Academy." Chapter 3 is devoted to Maria and Tita, together and separately, and chapter 4 focuses on Kareem. In both chapters on the students, I read their writing closely—in the manner of a sensitive literary critic or a concerned letter-reader—looking for the revealing phrase or grammatical knot or eloquent absence that betokens stories emerging or suppressed, contradictory emotions frozen in conflict, neighborhood institutions casting their light. Interviews and conversations with the students also help flesh out the world I understand them to be representing in their prose. As with any literary rendering, my readings say as much about me and my own conception of the world as they do about the students themselves and their worldviews, but I hope the students' voices and my own combine to form a compelling music.

The other major thread involves a theoretical consideration of authority and double-consciousness in writers, especially writers from groups that have historically been marginalized in U.S. society. In chapter 2, I define *authority* in terms of social institutions rather than individual authors. My claim is that authority is not a psychological quality or a textual attribute but a social phenomenon, and that authors derive their authority from identification with institutions that sponsor writing. In the chapter 5, using a passage from W.E.B. Du Bois's *The Souls of Black Folk* to contemplate what Du Bois calls "double-consciousness," I picture student-writers from marginalized communities within a drama of social transformation. I argue that many "basic" writers can best be seen as writers struggling to become authors. To become authors, all writers—including those who struggle with the conventions of standard written language—must learn to derive authority from public institutions like the academic disciplines or the work world. At the same time, authors-in-the-making may also benefit from learning to represent private institutions like family structure or neighborhood history. Writing teachers can, in essence, become developmental partners with their students, lending school authority to students while also helping students take on authority derived from institutions in their home communities.

I will not bore the reader with the arcana of my specialty. Those who know the literature on composition that has grown up in the last twenty-five or thirty years will recognize what theories and research I have drawn on here. They will see that, in general, I fit into that group of compositionists who view writing in its social context, who see writing not only as an individual act but as a process always situated within a universe of audiences, other texts, institutional demands, and group conflicts. For my discussion of authority and double-consciousness, I have also drawn much intellectual and moral support from works in educational anthropology, literacy ethnography, the sociology of knowledge, sociolinguistics, contemporary poetics, and literary criticism. Instead of a literature review, however, I depend largely upon my bibliography at the end of the book to provide an indication of what sources I used. It may be paradoxical for a social theorist not to highlight the network of names and publications upon which his work depends, but our field has grown large enough that sometimes the listing of antecedents becomes itself an antisocial act, hostile to the reader who just wants to get on with the story. I try in this book to oblige the general reader while not shortchanging the specialist.

Perhaps the simplest way of explaining my ambition for 'Round My Way is to call it a version of Mina Shaughnessy's Errors and Expectations, written after composition's decade-long enthusiasm for the socialness of written language. Shaughnessy showed in her book that the errors underprepared city college students made in composition were not random or willful or marks of inadequacy. In this book, I shift the focus from mechanics to rhetoric and use social context as an important factor in the analysis. But, like many others who write about "basic" writers, I share with Shaughnessy the purpose of deepening the composition teacher's interpretive power for the sake of people who want their voices heard in the American conversation.

I focus so much attention on three individuals because, despite my allegiance to a social view of composition, I believe that we should not lose sight of the individual writer. What I like about stories is their insistence on remaining distinct and unique even when we want to read them as representative and abstractable. Thus, I do not claim that Maria, Tita, and Kareem are "types" to be found in city schools. They have peculiarities and preoccupations that prevent them from "standing for" anybody else. When I write about their writing, I am trying hard to recover the texture and tone of their characteristic concerns so that the reader can fully appreciate the richness and conflicting forces out of which their written words emerge. For this reason, I sometimes think about this book as a nonfiction novel.

Had I chosen to write about three other students in my class at Neighborhood Academy, the book would contain a markedly different set of stories. There was Katina, a regal young African-American woman who was paying her own way through Neighborhood Academy; her mother did not see why Katina had left public school in the first place. Katina graduated at the top of her class, but she had a very difficult time writing anything more personal than a summary for history or an algebra problem set. She is, at this writing, in her third year of college, studying finance and marketing. There was Roberto, a Puerto Rican guy much loved by his friends and teachers, who wanted to be a marine biologist but doubted he could go to college. He is now selling drugs on the street corner, an occupation he swore he would avoid. There was Lynette, who came from a deeply troubled family and had a history of slipping into a towering rage at the slightest frustration. She became pregnant during the school year, but still managed to complete the prerequisites for nursing school and graduate with a scholarship to a two-year college. She is currently working toward her nursing degree. If I had room for a dozen more tales, the students of Neighborhood Academy could easily fill the pages—and each story would have its distinctive combination of tragedy and achievement, comedy and horror, inevitability and surprise.

But, of course, I am not arguing that we cannot generalize at all from accounts of individual writers. Certainly there are kids in the cityscape (and maybe the country, too) who are like Kareem, Tita, and Maria. I feel fairly certain that a significant portion of the social and family challenges my students faced in 1988–89 is shared by many, many other young people. I expect other teachers will recognize elements of character (or my rendering of character) in the students they teach. My account of these three writers, and the theoretical issues their writing suggested to me, must depend for its validity not on any claim for scientific rigor or ethnographic thoroughness, but on the vividness of the portraiture and the quality of attention the students and I have managed to apply to their own words. Like a poem, this book can not finally prove anything. Like a work of literary exegesis, it does not exclude other readings of the texts. Its primary virtue is in the fierceness and tenderness of its images—the ones Tita, Kareem, Maria, and I have collectively conjured.

This book tells a tale about me as a teacher and a reader at least as much as it offers an account of the texts and talk of three students. Some may wonder if I have not taken too many liberties with the students' words, or fear that I have appropriated the students' stories to make my own. Mary Louise Pratt's work on anthropological ethnography and travel writing stands as a reminder to me that I cannot resign my own place as a representative of the United States' dominant culture even though my sympathies are with those most hurt by that culture. A great many texts written or spoken by the students appear here. Still, it is always finally my voice which connects, elaborates, highlights, and unifies the narrative. I met and worked with these students in what Pratt calls a "contact zone," a social space "where disparate cultures meet, clash, and grapple with each other, often in highly asymmetrical relations of domination and subordination—like colonialism, slavery, or their aftermaths as they are lived out across the globe today" (*Imperial Eyes* 4). In the process of telling my readers about Maria, Tita, and Kareem, even if I use "their own words," I convert their experience into a narrative that takes its clarity and pointedness from my view and position within the dominant culture. And, as Pratt points out, narrative about a "periphery" serves to define the inquiring culture in ways that the narrative and narrator often blindly ignore (6). I try not to ignore my place in the telling, but I believe the story needs to be told nonetheless.

City schools are a "contact zone" in which I lived only on the teachers' side. In one reading of this project, then, I have written a travel book about my sojourn at Neighborhood Academy, with all the attendant pitfalls of that genre. The fact that I was a teacher as well as a researcher, however, gives the book perhaps a bit more of an engaged edge than the usual traveller or observer's report might have. Yes, I was concerned about the problems of initiating students into a dominant discourse, as I think my last chapter makes clear, but for a myriad of reasons I felt committed to doing the job. I have tried to resist giving the impression that my interpretations will provide readers with the "truth" about a set of "subjects." In defense of my method, I can only say that teachers in any environment must always act upon the conceptions they have of their students. Our ability to help people learn depends upon our ability to form images of students that are complex enough to allow for their capacities, but not so complicated as to prevent us from responding appropriately, even boldly, to their needs. *'Round My Way* shares my working knowledge about three young people I puzzled over and worried about and loved. My hope is that the following chapters provide a story other teachers can use to enable students to compose as authors.

Because this is, finally, a personal story about a teacher reading his students' work, I must tell you a little about how I came to meet the students at Neighborhood Academy. I began teaching in a precursor to the school in 1977. I had left medical school in search of a more congenial occupation for a writer and tried earning my living as a carpenter, an art school model, and a worker in a children's book warehouse. Nothing seemed to pay me much or to give me much emotional sustenance or time to write, so I decided I would try teaching school. I had no certificate to teach, no experience as a teacher or even a camp counselor, and I was still a bit shaggy and antiestablishment from my college years. None of the prep schools in the area had an opening for me, and, as a Jewish boy, I did not even think to apply to the Catholic schools. One day I happened to notice an unhighlighted line in the Yellow Pages for "The Neighborhood School." It might have been a tiny sectarian elementary school, but I decided to drive by anyway and check it out. I found a ramshackle building with holes in the porch and a front hall in need of paint and new flooring. Teenagers of all colors danced to disco in a lounge furnished with church pews and couches whose rips were only half-hidden by Indian-print fabric throws. It was a picture of a hippie free school, the like of which I had not seen since my days in San Francisco.

To my surprise, the lady at the desk near the door recognized my name and said, "Come in! I was just about to call you for an interview." My resume had apparently been forwarded to them from another school that had gone belly-up since I had sent out inquiries. The next thing I knew I was giving eight kids a talk on digestive enzymes in a kitchen experiment class, and a week later I had been hired as the science and math teacher at Neighborhood School.

I taught there for two years. During that time both the population of the school and the educational philosophy changed significantly. It had started as a Summerhill-type 1960s school established to educate the children of white, well-educated, alternative-lifestyle parents who lived in the immediate area of the school building. But, early on, it had also been adopted by a social service agency with a mission to serve runaways and troubled youth. Low-income students and their parents in West Philadelphia—unhappy with the public school system—began to hear about the school through friends and relatives who had attended. Meanwhile, the hippie contingent had moved out or shifted lifestyles. By 1979, the student population was nearly all black and largely dependent on some form of government aid.

The smile-if-you're-into-it attitude and the ungraded, unstructured classroom practice that had been the hallmark of Neighborhood School seemed less and less appropriate for students who had extremely poor school skills and little academic motivation. There was too much truancy and class-cutting, too much pot smoking, and too little learning going on in the school. I taught science with great energy (and no equipment), but I had the strong suspicion that the nobility of the project was not necessarily matched by an increase in knowledge or life-preparedness on the part of our graduates. My students in Human Sexuality were enthusiastic spectators throughout my lectures (I once performed a sex-change operation on a paper bag) and participated eagerly in discussions, but many girls got pregnant and boys got girls pregnant; one girl left the school and became a prostitute. I taught algebra and basic math and geometry mixed with digressions about how folks in other parts of the country lived, what Plato said about Forms, the nature of class in the United States, what jobs and training programs and college could mean for them in the future. But our best students never scored above 800 combined on the SATs, and all the progressive education in the world was not going to manufacture more entry-level jobs for Philadelphia's working class. We had a fair number of success stories—at least we thought so—yet we did not really know why we succeeded when we did, and we could not find funding sources who would listen to our stories anyway. Our greatest strength was that we cared about our kids, talked about them as a staff all the time, and tried very, very hard to make the course work personally meaningful to the students.

During the 1979–80 school year I left the country to travel in Mexico and Central America. When I returned in August 1980, I heard that the school had been taken over by another principal and that he had been "given" Neighborhood School by the sponsoring agency. This guy, whom I will call "Anthony Marioni" to preserve the anonymity of the school, had worked for years in the Catholic schools, but he also knew about alternative education and inner-city problems. He was supposed to be tough and caring at the same time, and savvy about the politics of the city. I called Tony up and asked him if he needed a science and math teacher. He hired me over the phone.

I did not know at the time Tony hired me that Neighborhood Academy—he had changed the name to make it sound a bit more respectable—had no money to pay the electric bill, let alone teacher salaries. The original sponsor, an independent agency with money problems of its own, had decided the school was just too hard to fund year after year. Rather than close the school cold, Tony convinced the agency to hand him all the desks, books, and equipment (a couple of basketballs, a cabinet full of preserved animals and old lab chemicals, one office typewriter that worked). The sponsor's final gift to the school was legal help to incorporate as a nonprofit entity so that we could apply for grants. The school had no income except that which came from the small tuition kids paid to attend. We held a short-term lease on the third floor of a half-abandoned hospital (the weekend we moved out of the old building, the art teacher returned for some supplies just in time to shut down the malfunctioning oil furnace before it blew up the whole block). It was not much to work with, but it had a core of students and a dedicated staff of four, and somehow we got through the first year.

This book is not about Neighborhood Academy and how it grew. Any school history will be rich in stories about characters, disasters, triumphs. That goes double for a chronically underfunded school devoted to educating students with histories of truancy, poor grades, family problems, neighborhood conflicts, and all the other risks and run-ins that go along with being on the work-and-welfare end of contemporary America. I will have to let Anthony Marioni write his own book on the subject. Suffice it to say that Tony and the rest of us taught forty, then sixty, then a hundred kids each year, despite heat shutoffs, a sudden forced move to an abandoned warehouse during a bitter winter, and constant financial crises that meant a scandalously low budget for supplies, equipment, and salaries. The school continued to grow and solidify its reputation as a place that could help kids who had not succeeded in the public schools. It survives today largely as a contractor for the Philadelphia School District. Its budget remains low and its facilities do not rival the University of Pennsylvania, but Neighborhood Academy continues to graduate students and send many of them off to jobs, the military, trade schools, and college.

I left the school in 1983 to pursue a doctorate in English at the University of Wisconsin. After five years in Madison, and a shift from modernist poetry to composition studies, I decided to write my dissertation about student-writers from marginalized groups. My wife and I wanted to return to Philadelphia, so I called up Tony and asked him if he could give me a job. We worked out the details by which I would teach a special English class for college-bound students, using them both as subjects and coinvestigators in my own project while also teaching them writing and literature. In addition, I would begin to develop a writing center, help out in college counseling, supervise new teachers, and substitute for absent faculty.

By the time I returned to Neighborhood Academy, it had become an institution of 130 students in grades seven through twelve with five teachers covering basic subjects plus Spanish and gym, two administrators, and a secretary (an Academy graduate who lived across the street). Located in Philadelphia's largest Puerto Rican neighborhood, the school draws students from many sections of the city. About half the students are black and half Puerto Rican, with a few white kids every year. The population is always almost evenly balanced by gender. Openly homosexual students have at times been prominent citizens at the school, and the staff has always worked to minimize homophobia as well as other forms of discrimination and group conflict. The families of most of the students receive some kind of public assistance, and nearly all the students had been enrolled in public schools before they found their way to Neighborhood Academy. Students pay a tuition significantly lower than the Catholic schools charge, and the rest of the operating expenses of the school are provided by the school district and (for a few years) city council, with some capital help from private foundations. The fight for funding continues, but, at the moment I am writing this, circumstances are a bit more stable than in the old days.

The school is "alternative" in the sense that it provides smaller classes than Philadelphia public schools typically offer, and curricular decisions are made by classroom teachers rather than by supervisory experts. The curriculum is not notably experimental or nontraditional, but the staff attempts to tailor and pace the course material to the needs of the students. The program as a whole is meant to take into account the circumstances that affect the school performance of each student. The staff meets once a week, and the greatest portion of their weekly meeting is devoted to discussing individual students.

The students experience the school as a caring and safe environment, and as a result they often thrive in ways they never had in larger and more bureaucratic settings. As one student I will call Kenny P. wrote me in 1989: "Neighborhood Academy to me is more than just a school. When home is hell and when suicidal thoughts cloud regular thinking there are people who care. When you feel like your alone in the world A hundred twenty five of your peers make you realize your not." His testimony is above all a tribute to Tony and the staff, who have made Neighborhood Academy a place where it is cool for teenagers to care about each other.

Neighborhood Academy students are very like their friends who attend public schools, except that for most of them a history of truancy and lack of school achievement prompted someone in their lives—a parent or grandparent, a teacher or counselor, social worker or parole officer—to seek a more individualized school program for them. The range of skill and ability levels at the school is dauntingly wide, but most students read two to six grade levels below their expected age-level performance. A significant percentage of Neighborhood Academy graduates go on to college or post-secondary training, largely because the teachers start early to help students formulate post-graduation plans, and the teachers work aggressively to see that their students get into programs that suit them. I can not say that Neighborhood Academy students are representative of all urban high school students, but they are hardly atypical. They face the sort of problems many urban students face, but they have the advantage of belonging to a nurturing community that over time can help them help themselves.

My special English class in 1988–89 was meant to prepare students for college work. The school staff chose for my class ten kids who had math and verbal abilities that made them likely college candidates. In addition, the ten seemed to have attitudes toward school that were positive enough that they might want to continue in an academic track after graduation. I found in the first weeks that only two or three of the students had thought seriously about going to college, but they were all eager to be challenged and to find out what they could do.

The class content was roughly centered on nineteenth-century American literature, with an accompanying theme of writing assignments meant to encourage exploration of the students' home communities. I asked for a fair amount of writing and reading from them, and we spent much class time discussing student and literary texts. My goal was to teach them to take responsibility for their ideas and to recognize that ideas and ways of expressing them could matter to them as a collective. We grew close as a group that year and eventually used our cohesiveness to reach out to the school and beyond. Our final projects included a yearbook for the school and a booklet of interviews with interesting characters from the students' neighborhoods.

Out of all the students whose work I collected and whose spoken words I recorded that year, I chose Tita, Maria, and Kareem for this study, not because they were representative but because I felt I could present the most rounded picture of them as writers. Kareem and I spent time together outside class, usually discussing his school problems. I also lived ten blocks from his house, so I knew his neighborhood. Maria and Tita spent even more time hanging around after school and talking with me. While Kareem was always wary of my taping our conversations, Maria and Tita did not mind having the tape player running during some pretty intense talks about life in their neighborhoods.

Other members of my English class were equally interesting writers and personalities, and some of them faced personal circumstances more trying than the ones portrayed in these pages. I interviewed students outside the class as well, and collected at least one or two pieces of writing from nearly every student who attended Neighborhood Academy during the 1988–89 school year. Yet when I sat down with my files and tapes, the stories of Kareem, Maria, and Tita emerged as the ones I wanted to tell. Kareem appealed to me because of his secrecy and the terseness of his writing. In contrast, the material I had from Maria and Tita seemed to assemble itself because they had worked so closely with me and talked to me so freely about their dreams and fears.

I would like to introduce the following chapters with a story about a student who was not in my college-prep class. I tell the story because it is a brief and self-contained tale about authority in writing, and yet, like all the stories in this book, it is incomplete—the on-goingness of lives is what prevents us from seeing them as exclusively tragic or happy or illustrative of an abstract principle. Moreover, I like the way the story represents Neighborhood Academy students simultaneously as special cases and as kids like all others. I found that to be sensitive to their particularity was the most effective way for me to accept their common humanity.

The student in question is Kenny P., the young African-American man who praised his school in the passage I quoted above. He was seventeen years old and had mild cerebral palsy. He used a crutch sometimes and spoke with a slight slur, but he could walk unaided and was not shy about speaking up in class. Kenny came to me for help in writing an English paper about being disabled, and the two or three brief sessions we had together remain with me as some of the most hopeful moments in my six years at Neighborhood Academy.

I present here a transcript of a conversation Kenny P. and I had, as well as a text of the paper he wrote after our chat in the writing center. I typed the conversation into the computer while we spoke. Both of us could see the transcript growing and Kenny could object if something I wrote down misrepresented what we had said—and he could take his answers to my questions home for use in drafting his paper. I have chosen to quote at length without interruption; I think the transcript will give the reader a flavor of the sort of talks I often had with students at Neighborhood Academy. Kenny's struggle to speak, apparent in his words here, can serve as a prelude to the longer dramas enacted in the student-centered chapters. I hope Kenny's story will show that combination of hampering factors and pure potential that I felt from Neighborhood Academy teenagers in nearly every encounter.

Kenny was not a very confident writer, nor had he ever had much success at school. His home life had not been too happy, and he had been in trouble with both the law and other students in a previous school. He had been in Neighborhood Academy less than a semester when we worked on this paper about "being handicapped." His English teacher had offered him this assignment as an alternative to another assignment Kenny had not turned in, and he really wanted to do this one right. But Kenny had no idea how to get started. We met first and talked about the assignment, what "handicapped" meant, how he could write without self-censorship in an initial draft. The following day, we met again. Although I had asked him to make at least a few notes on the topic, Kenny had written nothing at home—he said it had been too hard. This is how our conversation went on that second meeting:

> Kenny: I don't know whether to write to them [the class] or to write a story like put personal experience in a story.
> Eli Goldblatt: Who would *that* be written to?
> Kenny: I don't know. It's like my journal, to myself.
> EG: Why is it so hard to write to yourself?
> Kenny: That's the thing—its not hard to write to myself. It's hard to write to the class.
> EG: Why?
> Kenny: Because that's where I keep thinking if it's good enough. When I'm writing to myself I'm just writing the word I'm thinking. It's easier to write what you do during the day than to tell a story.
> EG: What story?
> Kenny: In general, if you had to write a story.
> EG: Like what?
> Kenny: Like you and your best friend going somewhere.
> EG: That's harder—why?
> Kenny: 'Cause you writing to a audience—that's why it's hard.
> EG: Any audience is hard? Even a good friend?
> Kenny: *No,* not a friend 'cause he knows you.
> EG: What makes the difference?
> Kenny: 'Cause the person know how you are—
> EG: In what sense?
> Kenny: In the way you think and how you talk.
> EG: Why is that an advantage?
> Kenny: 'Cause if you're writing to a friend it's like you're talking to him.
> EG: So?

Kenny: But everybody ain't my good friend.

EG: What would other people do to you if you wrote the way you spoke to a good friend?

Kenny: They would criticize if they didn't like your words.

EG: In what sense?

Kenny: They'd be like, "Oh he can't talk right."

EG: So what?

Kenny: I don't like that. Don't like to be criticized.

EG: Why?

Kenny: Because people criticize that means they think they're above you and nobody's above nobody.

EG: Nobody is above anybody?

Kenny: Nobody, only God.

[Digression about audience, from EG]

Kenny: Another thing—I don't got no friends in that class.

EG: How does that affect things?

Kenny: A lot compared to last year's class. I was friends with everybody. It was like family.

EG: Was it easier to write to them?

Kenny: Yeah.

EG: How much did you actually write to them?

Kenny: A lot. That's all I did—when I talk in class I pass notes.

EG: So not formal assignments but notes behind the teacher's back?

Kenny: Of course, I don't want to get in trouble. Talking about handicaps is a big pity story—just a big sad story.

EG: So how is that hard?

Kenny: I mean the little stuff they do everyday, when a handicap person do it it's big, real big. But it's like when you're handicapped, it ain't no really such thing as the word *disabled*.

EG: What do you mean?

Kenny: 'Cause *handicapped* mean just to find different ways to get around obstacles in your daily routine. That's what it means. If you couldn't run you find a way to run or you find your own way of running. And it's like everybody in the world has to earn their respect as a . . . like a person but when you're handicapped you have to earn the same respect and then some. And just to prove that you're normal and it's like the proving never stops. That's it.

EG: What's it?

Kenny: That's all I think about being handicapped.

EG: *All?*

Kenny: And you don't know who your friends are. I wonder every day if the people who shake my hand are my friends or they just feel sorry for me. Or they just be my friends 'cause I got money and everything.

EG: Does that mean you have to have money to have friends?

Kenny: Naw. But it's like you have to have something they like just to accept you. Like I wouldn't be accepted if I didn't wear the clothes I wear. I have to buy designer clothes so they won't look at my crutches.

EG: Yeah?

Kenny: That's it. That's what I think.

EG: That's *all* you think?

Kenny: Yup.

EG: Nothing else?

Kenny: Just one more thing. I be mad all the time.

EG: Why?

Kenny: Because I see my friends—little stuff like walk with a bookbag or smoke a cigarette and walking at the same time, and I can't even do that. That's it. That's absolutely it.

EG: You don't think about *anything* else?

Kenny: Nope.

When I presented this transcript to a group of people in a session at a conference on composition, a woman remarked that Kenny's comments on facing criticism and writing to an audience sounded like herself talking to her advisor about why her dissertation was going so slowly. Everyone in the session laughed, presumably because they too recognized the conversation. I think she was right in identifying the classic quandary of the student at any level: who is my audience and will they think me good enough? The teacher always stands between the writer and any other readers, even in the most enlightened classroom. But Kenny reveals another problem: facing criticism is different in school than it is on the street. Kids can surely be critical anywhere, but only in school are you required to open yourself up to scrutiny in front of your peers with no control of the setting for response.

But I think this conversation is about more than audience. It is about discovering a means to speak from a position of power. It is not so much that Kenny did not know his audience. I know from substituting in his English class that Kenny could write notes with the best of them, and in fact tried to cultivate alliances in his new school by exuberant displays of the "underlife," Robert Brooke's word for the note-passing and behind-the-teacher's-back whispering of classroom culture. But, at the time, Kenny P. was the only student with a physical disability in Neighborhood Academy. To speak to his classmates about finding "different ways to get around obstacles in your daily routine" meant representing to his peers a vision of reality they did not share. I am sure his language to me was permeated by expressions he had picked up from social workers and counselors he had encountered over the years, for the combination of his cerebral palsy and his troubled home life brought him into contact often with health and welfare professionals. Their language would include Kenny in a way that school language would not. But among the kids of Neighborhood Academy there must have been precious little acknowledgment of Kenny's crutches or his speech at all—silence would have been the polite response to his "handicap." I believe Kenny was hard put to tell his story in school, where there was little institutional authority to back up his words. What I did in this situation was to ask him to talk to me, and then I handed him the transcript of his words. I helped make the language of his private experience official in his school life.

My favorite line in the conversation is: "Just one more thing. I be mad all the time." It reminds me so much of the way we often suppress the emotions that both drive our need to write and hold us back from writing. Kenny faced a specialized sort of challenge in his personal and social context—no question that he had a harder way to go than I ever did—but he also confronted a predicament every writer must provisionally resolve again with each new project. When I was in college, my poetry teacher, who had published half a dozen books, once said to me in conference: "It doesn't matter how long you've been in this business. When it comes down to staring at the blank paper, you're standing on the same street corner waiting for the same trolley as everybody else." Kenny's troubles with "audience," with his power to speak about unmentioned experience, with how to represent a reality unseen by others, mirror frustrations common to all of us, especially when we have a personal stake in what we are writing.

After the conversation reported above, I suggested to Kenny a brief list of topics he could discuss in his paper, based on what he had said to me in the conversation about his ideas. The list went as follows:

Possible order of topics:

1. Definition of being handicapped
2. Earning respect
3. Friends
4. Little things for others are big things for us
5. I'm mad a lot

I said I did not know what he would do with the list or if he would find other issues he would like to discuss, but I urged him again to sit down and let it happen. I pointed out he had twice tried to shut down the conversation, claiming he really had nothing more to say, just when he was about to make a crucial statement. I told him he had a fine bundle of things to say now, and he better go out and say them. He came back the next day with the following essay:

If you Were like me.

What handicapp means to me. When a person says the word handicapp they would think something was wrong with that person Physicaly or mentaly. Some people would even try to be nice instead of hitting the word handicapp head on they would say disabled. I'm handicapp myself and I say being handicapp means that you have to deal with what's wrong with you and find different ways to get around obstacles in your daily routine, that's what I do everyday.

There is more things involed when your handicapp, but one very important part of being handicapp is earning respect. Everybody has to earn their respect weather it be from friends, Parents, or teachers, but when your handicapp you have to earn respect just like everybody else and then some. You have to prove to people that you can do the things that they do, and that's one thing that never stops.

Friends are also important. Everybody needs friends one way or another, but everybody needs friends. I wonder everyday if the

people who shake my hand are really my friends. I don't say nothing because that would be stupid to ask but I do wonder. It's hard
to tell weather your peers are your friends because they are or do
they just feel sorry for you. And that what no handicapp person
wants . . . someone's pitty.

I hate it when I see a person like myself on t.v. or on a show
like Jerry's kids. Certain people like fundrasers committees or
charitys try to get money to help handicapp people buy showing
you what the person can't do. When they find a little thing like
swimming they Hype it and get to everybody emotion. They
would say look this person has no legs only arms but he can swim.
Come on let's be for real not everybody knows how to swim but
most people do. The person with no legs just found a way to get
around that obstacle. The goal for everbody who can swim is to
enjoy the water, don't you think so.

Most times I'm mad because I'm the way I am. Because I see
the little things people take for granit like walking ans smoking a
cigerret at the same time. I wish I could do that. I can but I have
to ask my friend to hold my crutches. Nobody want to hold my
crutches while I smoke the cigerret that I asked for they might do
it but they really don't want to. And I hate to ask.

I wrote this because people tease me and I get hype weather
or not I'm quiet about it or not I still get hype when there's to
much teaseing. So don't call me crip anymore the name's Kenny
P. $.

I was pretty darn happy with this draft, and Kenny was beaming.
His mother had helped him with the final copy of the piece. This was
actually one of the major triumphs of the project, since Kenny and his
mom had an extremely explosive relationship, and his disability was
one of the most sensitive issues between them. I typed the essay into
the computer and he and I worked over the spelling and grammar—
although this was a clean piece of writing, for something this long and
rhetorically complex, with an excellent sense of paragraphing and only
minor sentence boundary problems. He substituted the opening phrase
for the title. Later, with Kenny's permission and his byline, I put "What
Being Handicapped Means to Me" in the first issue of *The Neighborhood Academy Journal* and passed out copies to everyone in the school.

Kenny was a celebrity for a few days and was pleased as he could be with himself.

This piece of writing draws on a number of institutional sources for its authority. It is first of all sponsored by the school, written both as a classroom assignment and as an article for a schoolwide paper. The essay successfully follows school language practices in its paragraphing and topic sentences and in the way Kenny follows the rough outline he worked out in conference with me. At the same time, by addressing his peers as the audience, by using slang like "hype," and by talking about smoking cigarettes, he announces that he is speaking as a representative of the culture he shares with his classmates. He also calls on the language of the contemporary social reformers who stand behind the latest civil rights legislation for disabled people. He wants to distance himself from elements of the established public view of "Jerry's kids," because—at least for Kenny—that institutional position cannot sponsor a writer to speak his mind, voice his rage, claim his commonness. Kenny P. here has, for the moment, transformed himself from a writer to an author by representing himself and his reality along institutional lines that will have power within his social setting.

I do not present Kenny P.'s disability, and his struggle to frame its interpretation by others, as merely symbolic. He is a real kid who said some unsentimental things about his friends, his crutches, and his self-respect. But some of the issues he raises are ones that do reflect special problems that Kareem, Maria, and Tita share. For all of them, the crucial issue is how to attain the kind of authorial presence necessary to explore and represent personal and community reality through written language. The struggle to become an author in this sense is the major focus of 'Round My Way.

This story, like all the stories in this book, can have no real ending because it is more about continuation than resolution. Unfortunately, the year after I met him, Kenny was kicked out of Neighborhood Academy for bringing a gun to school—a cardinal sin in the Neighborhood Academy rulebook. I did not know where he was for a few years. Recently, I met him on a busy city street as he waited for a bus. He had been in trouble for a while, but when I last saw him he was back in public school on a special schedule, working part-time for the school and taking vocational education courses. I cannot tell you if he will earn his diploma, find a job, live a happy life. But for one moment in his career—and mine—he and I watched words shape a reality he felt, and he brought that reality to light for others. I hope he will never forget that moment. I'm writing this book as a hedge against my forgetting it. If the following chapters are about anything at all, they signify an attempt to remember by telling stories. To me, that is the essence of my project.

2

. . . . . .

Authority in Its
Social Context

The stories and writing in the following chapters will probably serve to distinguish, in the reader's mind, the Neighborhood Academy students from their wealthier peers in condominiums, ranch houses, and farms throughout the United States. In this chapter, however, I want to focus on a dynamic of composition that all writers must engage: the struggle to be authors. I look at what power relations lie behind the fairly standard way "authority" is used to describe writing—the quality of ease and knowingness we recognize in respected writers from any field. As readers, we can usually sense when an author knows he or she has something to say and an audience who will listen, and we impute that sense to the individual writer. My interpretation of Maria, Tita, and Kareem's writing depends heavily upon a more social interpretation of authority as an attribute in writing.

When we view writing as an essentially social activity, rather than an activity performed by individual talents of major or minor genius, authority takes on a new meaning. To me, authority is a function of the role a writer plays in bringing cultural institutions to life, and the source of authority is not so much in the writer or the writing as it is in the institutions that sponsor the writing. I make a distinction between a writer and an author, based on this focus upon institutional sponsorship. I propose that the author/writer distinction may be a useful context for reconsidering the nature of "basic" writing.

In an article discussing the politics of interpretation, Edward Said
gives us a succinct analysis of the process of attaining a "social identity"
as an "expert":

> You cannot simply choose to be a sociologist or a psychoanalyst;
> you cannot simply make statements that have the status of knowl-
> edge in anthropology; you cannot merely suppose that what you
> say as a historian (however well it may have been researched) en-
> ters historical discourse. You have to pass through certain rules of
> accreditation, you must learn the rules, you must speak the lan-
> guage, you must master the idioms, and you must accept the au-
> thorities of the field—determined in many of the same ways—to
> which you want to contribute. (7–8)

This sounds like the Wizard of Oz model of "thinkology," which
holds that learned doctors "have one thing you haven't got—a diploma." I doubt that Said means to reduce all academic training to a
musical comedy, but he is warning that the information and theory of
a field cannot be gotten innocently.

Just before my doctoral examination, I had lunch with a member
of my examining committee. I was going over my reading list with her,
trying to find out how detailed my recall of the books would need to
be to satisfy my examiners. "The important thing is to have an *attitude*
toward every book," she finally said, in one of the most clarifying sentences I ever heard in graduate school. So that was what my years in
classrooms were all about! I needed to exhibit the attitude of a specialist, one so steeped in the literature that I could handle other specialists' work with that mixture of familiarity and respect a carpenter
accords the tools and materials of the trade. To focus on detail was an
apprentice's occupation, an attempt to show the masters I had "covered
the material." But to pass beyond the journeyman's stage, I had to
demonstrate that I could comport myself as a master who knew the
contour of debate, knew what constituted a proof and what a bluff,
knew how to stand alongside other members of the constituting club.
An attitude toward each book—even the books I hadn't read.

I would contend that the attitudes I developed were not "mine."
Though they may be marked with individualizing content, in their general outline my professional attitudes are a complex result of years of
socialization. Even if I articulate the most radical or reactionary posi-

tions, my attitudes are largely borrowed rather than created anew, and they belong to the lending institution no matter how I might recombine or reshape them. I suspect that the extent to which a researcher can bring innovation or challenge to a field is strongly influenced by whatever socialization in other institutions that individual may have experienced—in my case, time spent writing and reading poetry, studying medicine, caring for my son, and working outside the academy. My nonacademic life has led me to approach certain standard university attitudes with a less-than-reverent skepticism. But, at the same time, I can not hope to maintain a rhetorical position as an outsider with the kind of initiation I received within my discipline.

It is central to my argument that we can not talk about modes of discourse without a principled accounting of the institutions that sponsor discourse. We can not talk about authors unless we recognize the institutions which have authorized them to write. Since writers must create their texts within the context of institutions—sometimes within the context of multiple institutions—authors must always fulfill two roles: they act both as *representers* of a socially shared and institutionalized reality and also as *representatives* of sponsoring institutions.

I use *writer* to refer to an individual composing a text, but I reserve the term *author* for the writer as seen in the social framework of power relationships and cultural institutions. My argument is meant to apply to any author of any text within a literate culture; it seems to hold for the letter-writer and journal-keeper, novelist, memoist, or explicator of texts. Even the poet, who is often the exception in composition theories, fits into this analysis. The question, as I see it, is not what genre or mode a writer chooses, but what institution the writing maintains or elaborates or challenges, and how the writer fulfills his or her role as an author within cultural institutions. It follows, as well, that a writer's authority in a society depends in large part upon the power and influence of the institution that sponsors that writer's authorship.

Scientists, poets, and newspaper editors are presumably in a radically different position as authors than are Maria, Tita, and Kareem. Experts and specialists "express" not only themselves but the institutions they represent, and readers look to them to find out what we as a society think about reality, emotion, news. No one reads the writing of Neighborhood Academy students to discover "what's going on" in the world. That is perhaps one of the most trying obstacles these student-writers face: they are far from being thought "authors" in any meaningful way, even by themselves. We can learn a great deal about the idea of authority by first looking at those who seem to possess that attribute, and then by focusing on those who appear to lack it. After considering what social institutions are, and how authors elaborate and maintain them, we will be in a better position to return to Neighborhood Academy and appreciate the task the students there face as writers, and as would-be authors.

The end of this chapter considers "basic" writers and authority. What do the power relationships inherent in the social practice of writing mean for the writer whose connection with the dominant institutions in the culture are the most tenuous and stressed? As David Bartholomae defines the label, "basic writers" are those "who are refused unrestrained access to the academic community" (146); their access to other institutions are often equally limited. Basic writers are marked not only because they are awkward in manipulating the conventions of standard written English, but because they are usually authorityless authors—individuals asked to pull off the impossible magic trick of conjuring opinions from the dust of dispossession. In the terms I discuss here, they are writers struggling to become authors.

When we consider writing instruction from the point of view of power relations, certain complications that have always existed suddenly come into sharper focus. It is not enough that students should feel good about writing down the language they speak at home. That was the goal in the 1960s move to protect "students' rights to their own language," and it had a certain well-meaning logic that I personally still respect. However, in the cold light of the post-Reagan years, it is clear that certain sorts of "home" do not represent a base of political power sufficient to get aspiring students either financial security or widespread respect. To pretend otherwise is politically naive and, finally, destructive to the students. In the best possible interpretation of college acculturation, we hope students will learn new languages so that they might encounter ideas and images that will enable them to live more fulfilled lives. But whatever our reason for contracting with students to teach them the conventions and subtleties of standard English, we cannot expect them simply to embrace the college dormitory as their new home. To ask students from marginalized communities to take on academic discourse as their own is to invite them into a world where they have no power, requiring that they check their former badges of power at the door.

As teachers, we must choose to make the invitation into the college world, since conditions are wretched for many who live on the margins of American affluence. The whole system can only change when its naturalness is challenged by the presence of "outlanders," as Patricia Bizzell has called basic writers (*Academic Discourse* 164). At the same time, we must always be aware of the forbidding nature of the job "outlanders" face. In asking students from marginalized communities to engage with the university and the range of institutions it prepares students to work and live within, we ask them to take on a whole world which has proved itself hostile to the very existence of their friends and family. Moreover, progressive educators stand ready to urge these students, who are already struggling with the sheer stress of shifting cultures, not only to succeed in the system but to change it—something progressives ourselves are hard-pressed to do.

Still, the human-made nature of the whole edifice offers some hope. Writing is an institutionalized but dynamic project, not a static and mystical means by which God elects His Chosen. To write well is to accept a challenge to participate in the institution sponsoring the writing, even if that institution resists the writer's contribution. As long as student writers of any background can learn to see writing as an active art, they have a chance of growing individually and altering institutions collectively.

Texts Elaborate Social Reality

Through language, we create the human world. Everything we recognize as an object, an event, or an idea is both abstracted from and integrated into its surroundings by language. Whether we look at a tree, a bridge, or a painting, we perceive and register these instances of reality through our knowledge of history, science, myth, and personal experience that is codified and made accessible by an elaborate and only partially conscious system of visual and verbal symbolization. Michael Halliday has called language "a shared meaning potential, at once both a part of experience and an intersubjective interpretation of experience" (2). We register meaning with words and reflect on that meaning using words and pictures that are drawn from a shared human vocabulary. Even in our most private use of words or images—pet names, secret codes, unnamed fantasies—the stuff of these locked-away meanings is the common material of words and images available to many other people. We have to work very hard to isolate vocabulary from meanings others might associate with common experiences.

Peter Berger and Thomas Luckmann call language "the most important item of socialization" (59), by which "man produces a world he experiences as something other than a human product" (61). By this they mean that we use language to tell children about the world "out there," and language (and the traditions it carries about "Nature" or "Mother Earth" or "dirt") frames our relationship to that world we perceive as not human-made. Language is central to the construction and internalization of knowledge, by which we "realize" the world both in the sense of making reality apprehendable and in bringing it into being.

Language serves not only to bring external reality into being for us, it also makes real the institutions we use to domesticate that reality. I mean *institution* here as Berger and Luckmann define it: a habit which must be formalized in order to be passed on to a new generation (54). An institution functions not only as a material representative of a store of knowledge, as universities do, or as an active enforcer and promulgator of society's rules, as governments do, or as a repository for moral and metaphysical teachings, as religions do. An institution may also be any nexus of categories "thickened" or "hardened" (59) by history and use—for example, journalism, science, literature, atheism. An institution offers to children and adults alike the comforting objective fact of human patterns. Berger and Luckmann observe that institutions exhibit the firmness of the parent explaining how things in a culture are done (59).

In a culture such as ours, written language serves this realizing function with silent but irresistible force. Writing is always done in the service of human institutions; whether it is a memo, an insurance accident report, or a diary entry, writing does more than just get things done. Each instance of writing is an expression of life lived within shared cultural boundaries. A memo or report must be cast in a certain standard form, addressed and copied to the appropriate people, and focused on only certain features of the writer and readers' reality. You would not complain in a memo to an associate about how you hate to get up in the morning and carbon copy it to your boss; nor would an aesthetically inclined insurance adjuster note on his report the sensuous swirls he sees in a bent fender. If a new job ever required you to have a card printed with your name and title on it, you will know the convincing quality writing can have about institutional life. Suddenly you are what the card says you are, and the institutional logo helps make it so. The old joke "I can't be out of money because I still have checks" is in many ways an expression of the officialness that writing conveys to the "capital" of personal experience.

We usually think of the diary form as individual and set apart from institutional prescriptions. Our cultural inclination would be to draw the line for social construction at the locked cover of the personal diary. Yet, personal writing is also strongly implicated in perpetuating habits of thought. A diary upholds and elaborates our particular culture's sense of self, love, personal suffering. Emotions are not overt institutions like the army or Major League baseball, but they are deeply suffused with an ideology promulgated and reinforced constantly by our literature, our advertising, our political rhetoric. Diaries, consolation letters, and notes of apology bring into our most intimate circle the habits of feeling our culture generally fosters. A diary allows us to reflect on day-to-day experience, but it also allows us to legitimize our reflections on them, to write down expenditures, disappointments, family relationships "the way they are." This function becomes apparent when you look back over a diary or journal from a distant part of your life. The language often seems overly dramatized and often formulaic, to the point of being comic. Yet the diary serves to make "real" a contemporary perspective. Personal writing puts a name and thus a social meaning on our private experience.

At the same time as writing confers an institutional validity to both our public and private lives, writing done by individuals effectively creates and maintains the reality of social institutions. Universities are obvious examples of institutions realized by writing. The bulldozers and gardeners scrawling a campus on the earth, the marching band spelling out FIGHT on the football field—these are impressive (sometimes fearsome) feats of literacy. But they don't serve as the concrete fact of a school's existence as much as the lectures, textbooks, student papers, office memos, campus publications, and diplomas do. Students may be involved largely with the "dummy run," as James Britton (104–05) called classroom assignments without purpose or audience, or they may be required "to admire and report on what [academics] do," as Bartholomae characterizes many college writing tasks (278). But within the economy of college life, papers and essays and tests represent the *productivity* of the institution. Along with reading, writing (and math, another sort of writing) is the "work" students complain to their parents about and professors get paid to evaluate. Think about the mass of writing required of professors to keep their positions—not only learned studies but comments to students, committee reports, lecture notes. Take away the buildings and you have a university in search of a home; take away the writing and a university is unimaginable.

Of course a university is also a complex of institutions as well. Hundreds of competing and overlapping institutions are initiating new members into their ranks constantly on university campuses, while at the same time universities substantiate the very existence of the member institutions themselves. This applies not only to traditional academic disciplines like anthropology and chemistry, but to economic systems such as capitalism and socialism, to large-scale organizing concepts such as the cold war and evolution, to modish models of farming and sexuality. The fact that a subject is taught in a university is evidence for its institutional existence, as well as an opportunity for large numbers of people to elaborate and extend the life of that institution. This is one of the sore points for those who think the college curriculum is too full of "fads" and "politically correct" trends—the argument about "cultural diversity" and what constitutes the "canon" is an argument about which institutions should have the privilege and legitimacy of being wrapped in the written language a university manufactures.

The fact that writing is central to the institutional existence of a university is not, however, unique to the academy. The governmental memo and the corporate report are also assertions that institutions exist, that they have a life in the world. Surely an individual lawyer may distinguish herself with a particularly well-crafted brief, but the thousands of briefs produced each day support the very existence of law as a cultural habit, just as journals support learned disciplines. Even institutions as seemingly concrete as ball-bearing factories or beet farms are hedged around by legal documents and technological manuals. The bureaucrats and invoice-preparers, the shipping clerks and receipt-signers constantly proclaim that their agencies, cooperatives, corporations, and partnerships are social realities. If every Bartelby on Wall Street "preferred not" to scribble for his company, corporations would fade into a dream of blank paper.

Writing serves the same realizing function within our most intimate relationships. Two people are married because their names appear together on a form at the city hall, but many other written signs soon follow: both names appear on the their joint income tax form; either one can sign a check from their joint bank account; junk mail comes for "Mr. and Mrs. O——," whether they share a last name or not. As many couples who have lived together before marriage can testify, those "little" signs of legal status can seem remarkably poignant or daunting, causing a catch in the throat or a double-take for the first few years after the wedding. Even well after the thank-you notes are written, there is the abiding fact of marriage in all the written paraphernalia of a life: a will written together, an X in the "married" box on an insurance application. Those who remain unmarried, or whose relationships don't fit the heterosexual model, may find those small signs of married people's legal status a constant reminder of their exclusion from the social register.

An editorial in the *Philadelphia Inquirer* Sunday magazine of August 27, 1989, offers us an unintentional commentary on how texts shape our world (Mann 1). The editorial refers to the cover story article about a controversy stirred up by a community paper called the *Chestnut Hill Local.* The fracas centered around the outspoken editor for the *Local,* a kindly looking, older woman on the cover of the magazine. *Inquirer* Editor Fred Mann notes that journalists from "prestigious papers" often dream of owning and operating a little local because of "an undeniable appreciation for the community press":

> With small-town tabloids and neighborhood shoppers, you aren't bringing down presidents or grabbing the national spotlight, but you are affecting people's lives on a visceral, reactive level. Write about war in the Middle East and people will read because they know it's important; write about a traffic light on their street corner or their daughter's college acceptance and they will cut it out and save it. It's an immediacy and significance many journalists yearn for.

Mann is naming the division of labor in newspaper institution-building. "Prestigious papers" construct the reality of municipal, national, and international life for their readers—many of whom will compose their pictures of that life from television, with newspapers filling in telling details and a narrow range of opinions. In this interpretation of their role, large-circulation newspapers and other broad-based media do not "educate the voters" as much as they paint the larger and more distant scenery before which our local and palpable life is played. The United Nations, the war in the Persian Gulf, and the trade deficit would not exist for most of us were it not for the "news." They hardly exist for us even so. I am not arguing that Congress and acid rain are not actual phenomena. However, given the vastness of our world, they don't exist in most daily lives without the realizing power of written language.

Painting the big picture, however, does not often touch the passions that local reality-building can set off. Articles about traffic lights and college acceptances draw personal experience into a wider social reality; thus, written text releases the emotions attached to the things of our day-to-day life as they pass into the shared social world. Local reports don't have the "consequence" associated with "world" events (we must assign distant events more prestige or else we wouldn't care about them at all; people read about them "because they know it's important"). But, for the community, local reports bring personal life into the social sphere and, at the same time, bring the social sphere into personal life—thus substantiating both as "reality." Local news doesn't usually receive television attention, so the community paper serves a very welcome function in making the local scene "real." The family, the neighborhood, the city, state, and nation all become nicely prioritized and arranged by the reading and viewing we do about them. Experience may constantly challenge those neat arrangements: a fire in your home will outshine OPEC oil price hikes, even if the distant news eventually will mean higher prices at the gas pump. Friendly editorials like Fred Mann's try to tidy things up again, the way one picks up a room after a party.

Experience—and talk about experience—would yield a very different picture of reality if we never looked at national news or local weeklies. Variations on everyday routines would be the large scale drama, set on the background of terrain we could see and hear and smell. We laugh at people caricatured as "hill people" who don't read newspapers. In the same way, sophisticated city people who go away on vacation are often ridiculed when they return for being "out of it," even if they return with a renewed "sense of themselves." People who depend on local gossip and the minister's sermon for their reality possess a knowledge no less institutionalized than does the typical urban newspaper reader, and those of us for whom the family debt looms larger than the national debt are no less free of the doleful legitimizing of written symbols. But for most middle-class readers, Mann is naming a genuine battle for the real world, fought on territories conjured, surveyed, and policed by the words we read or the words read to us.

This function of written texts to maintain and elaborate habits of mind and create or alter the institutional structure of culture can be seen in another light as "meaning-making." Reading theorists and writing theorists have stressed the way written texts must be decoded and composed in a meaningful structure. In a short review article, Colleen M. Fairbanks sums up research on basic writers like this: "These researchers all suggest that teachers focus on meaning—the meaning of the text and the meaning of the errors" (78). Focusing on meaning is sound advice not only for basic writers, who need to make sense of the texts they meet because all of us must. But in many ways textual meaning is exactly this same process of institution maintenance and elaboration I have been discussing.

What we read makes sense to us because it becomes associated with categories and scenarios that we "know" as the shaping institutions of our lives. No datum, no schema, no image has any meaning if it is not attached to the web of human habit. This web is not natural in the sense of a spider's biological product, nor is it an "ecology," as Marilyn Cooper describes it. It is emphatically nonnatural, an artifact of the human need for culture. Of course, the status of meaning as human-made makes it no less necessary or compelling, but the distinction is important because it emphasizes the extent to which our notions of "common sense," "meaningful exchange," or "incomprehensibility," are context dependent, relative, and vulnerable to all the toxins that humans manufacture out of race, class, gender, and other differences among people.

The meaning a text makes is determined by the extent to which it enlivens and is enlivened by a stock of knowledge available to the writer or reader. This is, of course, E. D. Hirsch's famous argument in *Cultural Literacy*, but in the context of meaning as institution-building, we can see "cultural literacy" as an almost undisguised struggle for the primacy of institutions named, evoked, and realized by certain texts. Wolfgang Iser refers to the "horizon" experienced by the reader and asserts that the gap between the author and the reader's perspective of the world is what enlivens the reading act. But surely the ground for that struggle "to take over the author's unfamiliar view of the world" (Iser 97) is that reader and writer already share so many of the same assumptions about the world that any differences are negotiable. Thus, meaning-making is a process, in writing and reading, of coming to new realizations about institutional structures already present for the person composing or reading a text.

Writing, in short, establishes our most personal as well as our most public institutions within us at every turn, but of course the messages of standardized attitudes can be damaging and contradictory. Cultural critics have long pointed out the absences and distortions set up by the institution-building that goes on around us in print and image, the conceptions of love and history, body image and heroism that are installed in our consciousness through beer ads, children's books, and television dramas. To resist common conceptions of gender relations or sexual orientation or racial hierarchies means resisting the flood of institution-affirming printed matter that swirls around us. Occasionally voices can be raised against the common drift, but they succeed only when they gain the backing of a sizable countervailing institution. Protest against the Vietnam War, for example, only became effective when it had been bolstered by legitimizing supporters from within traditional church and political factions and had fully developed a social movement on its own which, by 1970, had achieved the status of a counterculture. How much harder to be a black or Latino teenage writer, standing in the institutional flood of the Bush economic "recovery," composing in the service of habits of mind and body far from the sponsorship of powerful institutions.

When readers and writers do not share a sense of social order, of institutional knowledge as intact and dependable, composition and interpretation are difficult or impossible. "Sharing" and "negotiating" sound like civil enough enterprises for readers and writers. However, people on either side of a text don't always come from worlds governed by the same rules and economic constraints, and when the gap is great trouble can develop. As I will discuss later in this chapter, this is the ground upon which students from marginalized groups struggle with authorship.

The Author's Role

Within the turbulent currents of meaning-making and institution-building, the author's job is far more complex than it looks. One sits down to write a letter, a journal entry, an article for the *Chestnut Hill Local* or the *Philadelphia Inquirer*, a paper for a class or an essay for a journal, a poem for the drawer or for a small magazine or a national weekly. A writer writes, and much has been written about purpose and audience and genre. Yet the role of an author is like any other social role, determined by and determining the character of the institution that fosters and depends upon it. "Institutions are embodied in individual experience by means of roles," Berger and Luckmann observe (74), and they picture a person in a role acting as a *type* rather than as an individual. What is more, through such typified behavior individuals "bring institutions to life" (75). Authors are perhaps the preeminent life-givers to most of the institutions in a literate culture.

We may at first resist the thought that the solitary novelist at work in her studio in Martha's Vineyard is a comparable figure to the Democratic ward leader handing out leaflets on election day. Yet our recoil reflects the prestige that embedded institutions have over overt ones. There is something crass about upholding a named institution by wearing its logo or handing out its literature. Talking up a party or a cause or a company sounds too much like cheerleading or boosterism. Developing ideological positions in scholarship or art—our picture of sexual relations, our image of "primitive" peoples, our attitudes toward the environment—is accorded the higher honor of serious and disinterested cultural work. Perhaps there should be some categorical difference made between the two sorts of institution-building. Yet they are not so conveniently distinct.

The ward leader works to maintain an explicit institutional structure while a novelist labors to test, elaborate, and transform our habits of thinking about history, relationships, landscape. If the novelist "succeeds," she may enter established literary circles, win prizes and acclaim. Perhaps eventually her work will be accepted as Literature—even if she has never left that solitary and hard-won room of her own. The ward leader may rise in the party, win elective office, give speeches on television, formulate national policy. Society will not similarly regard or reward the work the artist and the pol do, but they have more in common than either would readily admit. None of us can escape, even in our most intimate moments, from the social formations we live.

Martin Nystrand has pointed out the reciprocity implicit in the text's placement between writer and reader. Building on Rommetveit's observation that "we write on the premises of the reader and read on the premises of the writer," he has developed a view of the writer/reader relationship as interactive and akin to an electric circuit set up by the writer but completed by the reader (Nystrand, *Structure* 49; Rommetveit 63). Nystrand refutes those theorists who would assert the autonomy of the western nonfiction prose essay by saying that a "text is explicit not because it says everything all by itself but rather because it strikes a careful balance between what needs to be said and what may be assumed" (*Structure* 45). This model fleshes out the general conception of writing as a social act—laid out in the large-scale dialectic of individual and society by Karen LeFevre—but it does not adequately take into account power relationships between student:teacher, employee:employer, writer:editor, or, more generally, author:authorizing institution. I want to expand the view of the writing situation from a focus on writers and readers as individuals to the wider scene in which authors—even the most rebellious authors—play roles determined by institutional demands.

Edward Said says "no one writes simply for oneself," adding that "there is always an Other" (3). A writer's central function is to *represent* both a reality and an authoritative narrator to this Other, the reader, within some socially accessible institutional frame. Let me outline two important meanings the word *represent* has for authors. First, authors represent the "object" of their writing through description, explication, and plot, using the conventions available to them within a given style or genre or discipline. Simultaneously, though, authors offer readers a persona or voice that talks about the "object." This persona is the shaping "subject" of the discourse. The way the persona tells the story—the order of details, the attitude toward physical or emotional details, the tone of the prose—represent not only an individual but an institutional way of viewing the world. An author is one who presents a thing again (surely no "object" can be presented wholly new, for it must always be offered in language which has been used to present like things), but also an author is one who stands for a way of viewing the world which is more or less shared by others. An author is a *representer* and a *representative.*

For example, let's compare two ways of writing about the "Red menace" hysteria that grew up in the United States after World War II. Here is Samuel Eliot Morison from his *Oxford History of the American People:* "These efforts to 'root out' subversives from government, colleges, and even business, ruined the careers and reputation of thousands of patriotic Americans whose only offense was to have lent their names to some 'front' organization during World War II" (1074). Morison is angry at Senator McCarthy and his ilk for "ruining" careers. His tone here, as elsewhere in his history, is a masterful combination of the passionate spectator and the learned scholar. His phrases "even business" and "patriotic Americans whose only offense was to have lent their names to some 'front' organization" indicate that Morison speaks as a solid Democratic liberal who favors civil rights, holds business as a good engine for American prosperity, and regards patriotism as a virtue that can override youthful flirtation with radical causes. He is representing a picture of McCarthyism consistent with the views of his tradition, and at the same time he is modeling the tone and bearing of one who feels fully authorized to speak for his "people."

Now here are some lines from Allen Ginsberg's poem, "America," a piece addressed to the same general cultural phenomenon:

America it's them bad Russians
Them Russians them Russians and them Chinamen. And them
    Russians.
The Russia wants to eat us alive. The Russia's power mad. She
    wants to take our cars from out our garages.
Her wants to grab Chicago. Her needs a Red *Reader's Digest.*
    Her want our auto plants in Siberia. Him big bureaucracy
    running our filling stations.
That no good. Ugh. Him make Indians learn read. Him need
    big black niggers. Hah. Her make us all work sixteen hours a
    day. Help.
America this is quite serious.   (147–48)

Ginsberg positions himself outside the economic structure, satiriz-
ing not only the brute ignorance of McCarthyism but also America's
obsession with its industrial power. He seems positively clownish compared to the reasonable but compassionate persona of Morison. Yet
Ginsberg, in freeing himself from representing the liberal institutions
he wanted to implicate in the era's sins, melds Red-baiting with racism
and materialism to present a view of the era quite different from Morison's. Ginsberg represents the problem as moral and metaphysical,
sprawling all over our public as well as our private lives, while Morison
focuses on orderly and identifiable villains who preyed upon innocent
citizens.

Despite his intentionally nostalgic evocation in the poem of the
Communist Party, Ginsberg does not act as a representative of any
explicit institution in "America." But he is clearly aligned with a time-
honored American institution of the Opposition: the Wobblies, the
counter-culture, the "queer nation." He does present the Communist
party to the reader, but not in a way that would suggest his narrator
speaks for the party. He speaks for the America that America won't
recognize. No less than Morison, Ginsberg represents and elaborates a
reality that draws on a distinctive social base.

In the role as representer, an author displays, clarifies, and thus
interprets some aspect of reality in terms consistent enough with existing institutionalized ways of thinking so that at least some readers will
be able to incorporate the representation into their own picture of the
world. To represent a thing, an idea, an event is to render it visible in
the light of the contemporary world, to add it to or reinforce it within
our repertoire of the real. A third grader may represent a doll in a few
sentences written to the class. A literary scholar at a conference may
represent Nietzsche's concept of the "prison house of language" to
modernist scholars. In both cases, the writers demonstrate their skill in
manipulating the grammar, syntax, and diction expected by their readers when a thing or concept is presented. The third grader can't talk
about a doll to the class using the language of the Nietzsche scholar,
and a presentation done in third-grade syntax and vocabulary would
embarrass a literary audience. In either case, the comprehensibility of
the presentation—how it will elaborate or run counter to the common
stock of knowledge—requires that the author use words the audience
is more or less accustomed to. Perhaps one or two words will be new

to some listeners, perhaps even something about the presentation will surprise the audience, but both authors will build their meanings out of standard and assumed understandings about the nature of dolls or philosophy.

Representation, however, is not wholly dependent upon the explicit conventions of word choice and grammar. Categories matter, too. Dolls are classed among inanimate objects used for play by kids. A third grader who talks about a doll as a religious fetish capable of magical feats might upset the children and disconcert the teacher. A scholar who compares Nietzsche to the western tradition of buffoons and clowns would have the devil of a correspondence to answer afterward. Representations are possible outside the normal channels—witness Susan Leonardi's 1989 *PMLA* article discussing recipes, cookbooks, and novels together (probably the most refreshing article in that respectable journal for a decade, but it could only have appeared after feminism became firmly established within the Modern Language Association). Still, whatever new channel an author digs, it must eventually communicate with the existing waterways. Otherwise, the creek dries up or the whole plain floods (a metaphor can itself be just such an experiment in challenging categories). Every challenge to categories runs the risk of losing the power of representation.

It is as representatives that both the local newspaper writer and the national journalist "report the news." Out of such printed representations, readers build up the social reality we share with one another. We depend upon writers to bring the world to us in language, and the centrality of this function puts a much heavier responsibility on the writer than we normally recognize. Since we can never personally evaluate the dependability of all the authors we hear from daily, we often look to accrediting institutions for the trustworthiness of authors, not to the individuals themselves. We say, "Oh, there must be something to the story because it appeared in the *New York Times*" (more convincing than the *Philadelphia Inquirer*), or we peek into the program to see where the Nietzsche lecturer teaches and what books she has published. In the case of the third grader, the author's popularity with the class will have a powerful influence on the text's ability to add or detract from what the kids know about dolls or how they can talk about dolls in public. A kid who plays ball well or carries the right lunch box is usually influential with peers, and young children are particularly keyed to the power of sponsoring institutions like sports or the movie industry. Authors carry greater authority when they represent institutions we credit with greater power to shape and codify reality.

Representation depends for its "clarity" on being consistent with an *attitude* the audience takes toward the object being described. Knowing current attitudes is essential for authors, who must present themselves as acceptable spokespeople for sponsoring institutions. They can't bend or expand categories too far without losing precious social ground. If the third grader talking about dolls is a boy, in most American schools he can't be too enthusiastic, for fear that the kids will ridicule him (or what is worse, "write him off" completely as an authority on anything). In this instance, the sponsoring institution is not only the school and the doll industry, but the categories of gender in which third graders are already well versed. The scholar discussing Nietzsche must not write too casually about "dear old Freddy," especially if she is young and black, because she will be thought pretentious, silly, unprofessional. She is serving not only the explicit institutions of "higher learning" and her specialized field, but the overarching institutions of professional life and, as always, gender and race expectations. A jovial male professor emeritus, especially if he has a German accent and rosy cheeks, might well get away with the familiarity denied a young, black, and female scholar. This is not to say boundaries can't be transgressed and challenged, but nearly every challenge will be met with resistance. Even once boundaries are pressed, they shift slowly; usually they require mounting pressure from a sizable population of authors and their supporters before the lines of acceptable representation give way.

Similarly, authors are expected to represent the object of their discourse only within certain assumed social bounds. If the third grader describes his doll "pooping on the dining room floor," his parents might receive an urgent phone call from his teacher or the school psychologist. If the scholar refers to the way Nietzsche has made her redo her kitchen, she will have to prove her "critical move" reveals some profound insight; she could not simply mean that Nietzsche helped her with her decorating. Whatever oddities of attitude the representer offers, he or she must also offer enough contextualization (or others will offer it for them: "J—— has had problems recently with his little sister pooping on his toys"; "Professor M—— must be a feminist—why else would a woman dare mention a kitchen in a professional setting?") to make the writing seem "comprehensible" to readers.

Again, authors of literature are no less representers and representatives than third-grade show-and-tellers or professors of German philosophy. The poet who is thought "obscure" may remain so because the attitude and context of her writing is never adequately shared by a large enough group of people, and her representation of reality is never accepted as valid or effective. Social change may bring a poet into fashion. Readers recognize slowly that the poet was "ahead" of her time and had imagined a way of viewing the world that eventually was adopted by a number of people, particularly members of a dominant class (Emily Dickinson is one example). Scholars may build an explanatory structure around her texts so that new readers can accept her words as consistent with social knowledge (Gertrude Stein, for instance). Of course, publication with the right houses and awards from the proper associations supply authors with a great deal of goodwill from their reading public.

The attitudes authors must represent do not originate with them. Even in our most individualistic model of writing practice, we do not imagine that a third-grade boy's attitude toward dolls or a female professor's attitude toward Nietzsche represent purely private and exclusive feelings. In order for writers to have their words considered in any forum, they must have enough familiarity with accepted attitudes to be both representers and representatives.

Within this social context of institutional representation, the complex quality that combines the way the individual writer looks at the object and the audience, and the way the audience looks upon the writer, is the *authority* of an author. *Authority* is similar to the rhetorical concept of *ethos,* Aristotle's name for the character a speaker presents to the audience. Karen LeFevre takes *ethos* to "refer not to the idiosyncrasies of an individual, and not to a personal and private construct such as is often meant by 'personality'; rather, ethos arises from the relationship between the individual and the community" (45). Like ethos, authority is far less a quality of an individual than it is an artifact of the individual's personal and social relationship with the culture. I use the term *authority,* however, because it makes explicit the power transaction implicit in the writing situation.

This elusive quality of authority doesn't reside primarily either in

authors or texts. Authority is essentially derived from the power of institutions. Like the radio waves generated by electrical current, authority speaks through receivers most tuned to the institutional frequency.
The strength of authority we experience in the literary pronouncements
of T. S. Eliot or the judicial findings of a Supreme Court judge come
from a happy confluence of personality, ingeniousness of prose, and
the manifest concerns of powerful institutions at a given time. Certain
writers—through hard work, diligence, talent, birth, and breeding—
internalize the knowledge and manner of central institutions to such
an extent that they come to be quintessential representatives of the
culture's power. Although Eliot did not see the sociological implications of his definition of *tradition,* his famous pronouncements in "Tradition and the Individual Talent" do fit into the framework of institutionalized authority:

> Tradition is a matter of much wider significance. It cannot be
> inherited, and if you want it you must obtain it by great labor. It
> involves, in the first place, the historical sense, which we may call
> nearly indispensable to any one who would continue to be a poet
> beyond his twenty-fifth year; and the historical sense involves a
> perception, not only of the pastness of the past, but of its presence;
> the historical sense compels a man to write not merely with his
> own generation in his bones, but with a feeling that the whole of
> the literature of his own country has a simultaneous existence and
> composes a simultaneous order. This historical sense, which is a
> sense of the timeless as well as of the temporal and of the timeless
> and of the temporal together, is what makes a writer traditional.
> And it is at the same time what makes a writer most acutely con-
> scious of this place in time, of his own contemporaneity. (4)

Eliot argues that you cannot be traditional just by being born into
a culture. The writer works hard to attain this "historical sense" that
tunes "him" (and the gender here is important) to the concerns of the
past as they are manifesting themselves today and evolving in the future.
The profound problem with Eliot's version of authority is its eth-
nocentric tone. We can't all identify with the monarchy, the High
Church of England, and Milton. He doesn't see his sense "of the time-
less and of the temporal together" as an artifact of a single institutional

complex based on the dominance of the British Empire. His "historical sense" doesn't account for other "traditions"—nonwestern or female-centered or rooted in oppressive living conditions. For these reasons, his image of the poet momentarily stuns those of us whose traditional institutions are less imperial, whose historical experience involves being ruled rather than ruling. We wonder, at first, what authority we can claim. Of course in recent years feminists, African American and Latino writers, and many others who do not identify with dominant institutions have struggled to legitimize their own cultural institutions as the basis for authority in writing. Yet Eliot's picture of one sort of authority illustrates just how intoxicating and empowering it must be to identify so completely with an institution possessing great temporal might as well as intellectual wealth.

I don't want to suggest that a grand author's relation to cultural institutions is slavish. No "higher authority" told Eliot what to say; no conspiracy of corporate executives and politicians mandate their representatives to produce so many cubits of cultural reality. This was, in fact, the mistake of the literary bureaucracy under Stalin. They could not order great literature because the identification must come from within, must be a result of real conviction and determination. Merely to maintain institutional reality requires only that one understand the forms by which the institution asserts itself. Literature extends and investigates the forms of institutional reality, and therefore asks from its practitioners a much greater and more intimate knowledge of the "tradition" out of which the writer creates.

It would be tempting to compare authors to surfers who catch a powerful wave, surfers who only have the freedom to wear outlandish swimwear as long as they stay in the wave's pocket headed toward shore. Some popular and powerful wags in government and journalism are undoubtedly like surfers. But to apply that model to Eliot or Sandra Day O'Connor would only oversimplify the idea of authority. Such authors enjoy a freedom of expression and thought that is probably unequaled in any other quarter. More like composers whose works are commissioned by famous orchestras, they have at their disposal the finest instruments played with the highest skills the culture can provide. But like musical composers, their power to command respect and continued access to the instruments of culture-making depends on their ability to write a music that extends and even challenges institutional categories without threatening institutional foundations. The possibilities and directionality of institutions are far more various than the surfer's wave, but the ineluctable and impersonal power of the wave is very much like the wash of a culture's history.

A rebellious writer, too, often shares a good deal of common ground with the institution she rebels against, even if her authority is derived from her opposition to the institution she attacks. The power of her argument depends in large part on her understanding of the institutional realities she opposes, including its knowledge base, its standards for truth, and its definitions of visible and invisible objects. However, the key for a writer who rejects dominant institutions is to embrace and elaborate alternative institutions that will help foster a position, an image, a story that can appear new and vital on the stage once held exclusively by more established interests. Ginsberg, for instance, is drawing upon habits of protest and alternative response that had reached sufficient strength in his time. He could stand on the Beat ground to launch his poem, and it would be a complete misunderstanding of "America" to see it as the yawp of a lone dissenter.

One who is simply angry or bewildered or inarticulate in the face of an institution will either be flung out of the way, ignored, or gently brought within its bounds. When we talk about large numbers of students trying to succeed in a school system they don't regard as their own, we must recognize how Eliot's words ring as a motto of mockery, and the strength of alternative institutions is choked off at the schoolyard gate. Resistance without authority is inevitably silent or silenced.

Authority and the "Basic" Writer

The continuing problem of what to call "basic" writers suggests that these writers are a troublesome presence within the institution that sponsors their writing. Are they "remedial" or "beginning" or "disadvantaged" or "developmental," or are they merely "illiterate" or "slow" or "bad"? Basic writers—I will take the quotes off the term, though the conundrum of naming these writers persists—are difficult and costly to accommodate in the academic system. They require special courses and teachers trained to deal with their writing, which to an educated eye seems defective, sketchy, pointless—almost a caricature of "good" writing. They often experience college as a vast obstacle course and psychological torture ground, while "more prepared" students experience their college years as an emotionally charged rite of passage into adulthood. Basic writers have a hard time with college writing, and colleges have a hard time with them.

Basic writers also present a serious ideological challenge to the institution. If it weren't for them, however, the writing process would probably still be a transparent and relatively unremarked phenomenon. The rise of composition theory in the late 1960s and early 1970s is in large part due to the open admission policies of that time. Although much work in the area is no longer concerned with basic writers, it was their presence in the classrooms that first alerted large numbers of teachers and administrators that something about the writing process was deeply problematic. Many have quoted the grousing that historically went on about the poor writing skills of college students at Ivy League schools; however, these complaints did not lead to the massive contemporary effort to analyze the writing process. Only in the course of the expansion of the university system after World War II and the influx of black, Hispanic, Native American, Asian, and poor white students that followed the civil rights movement and the prosperity of the sixties did the writing process gain institutional palpability and substance as an object of study. The marginality of composition research and pedagogy is still probably due in part to the lingering stigma of transgression—if we hadn't let all those unwashed masses in the door, none of this composition theorizing would have been necessary. And the visibility of writing as an active process of legitimating the institution is deeply embarrassing to all those who would rather see knowledge as an objective human pursuit, a simple and noble quest for truth.

What is "basic" about basic writers is that writing for them involves a fundamental power negotiation with the institutions that live by and for writing. They hold tickets that admit them to classes and reserve rooms for them in the dorms, but the crucial question of their entrance into the discourses of college life revolves around whether or not they can see themselves, or be seen by others, as representing the institutions they are required to serve as authors-in-training. It is one thing to buy the sweatshirt of your school; it is quite another to be asked to think of yourself as a sociologist, an astronomer, or a literary critic. All the grammar lessons and etiquette instruction in the world cannot authorize a writer if he or she cannot imagine taking on the dual role of representer and representative in the institutional setting of college course work. And it becomes a real test of wills if the teachers themselves cannot imagine certain students as representing professional interests.

Basic writers are not different in kind from other writers. All writers must struggle to attain a sense of authority in their writing since all writers must adopt the authorial roles of representer and representative. Imagine, for instance, a senior writing an honor's thesis in economics. She is faced with the challenge of writing like an economist without an economist's training in standard attitudes'toward economic data, a familiarity with the debates between experts, a long-tempered faith that she can make institutionally acceptable sense out of the tangle of details and opinions she has unearthed in her "research." Or think of the graduate student in English who is asked to write a paper on Henry James's *The Ambassadors*. He's read all the critics and has what he thinks is a decent organizing idea, but he just can't form a coherent and forceful argument. Or yet again, picture a junior faculty member who must transform her dissertation into a book in order to gain tenure. Like the undergraduate and the graduate student, she feels blocked: will her argument, which worked so well for her committee, be convincing to the field at large?

Such cases are not isolated crises in self-confidence. Each of these writers is struggling to attain a modicum of authority to carry out a writing task. Their authority will be constituted by the stock of knowledge and panoply of attitudes they have developed over time within their institutionalized discipline, but the strength of their authority derives from the extent that they feel "authorized" by the institution to speak, to fashion the stock of knowledge in an original way (though of course always within the bounds set by the institution, or not far beyond). As authors, they must feel a sense of identity with the sponsoring institution itself, so that to elaborate institutional categories is a satisfying and personal goal for the writing. To function as an author, the writer must become more and more fused with the life of the institution itself and feel her or his "work" contributes in some way to the "body of knowledge"—the institutional substance—in the field. Writers need to feel a stake in their writing project, which in essence means they share some of the authority of the sponsoring institution as they carry out their writing task. At the same time, the authority of the institution itself grows as writers become authors, engaging to represent and realize the field as neophytes, acolytes, and eventually professionals.

To perform the act of writing and still be within the institutional circle is a trick of balancing assurance with transgression. Any act of writing, even the most conventional, requires some challenge to received knowledge—otherwise the texts already extant would simply suffice. Every writer must take the risk of joining a conversation whose topics, enthusiasms, and anathemas have been established by shadowy gray eminences whose power is the power of the culture itself.

What makes basic writers a special case is that their access to "authorization" is by definition restricted. The issue for them is not oral versus literate cultures, or restricted versus elaborated codes. As I mentioned earlier, Rommetveit observed that we "write on the premises of the reader and read on the premises of the writer" (Rommetveit 63), but for marginalized students the premises are always somebody else's. In the crudest street terms, the issue becomes: "Money talks and bullshit walks." Perhaps we should revise that saying to read: "Money writes what bullshit fights." Dominant institutions shape and control the neighborhood life of many basic writers, and writing offers little hope of sharing or challenging the power of those institutions. This is not an encouraging situation for a young, aspiring author.

To be sure, the students at Neighborhood Academy come from communities that have many strong institutions of their own. Despite all the horror stories in the papers, there still remains a strong—if embattled—sense of family in the neighborhoods. The churches in black and Latino neighborhoods still act as important sources of strength. Indeed, in a pair of studies, one focusing on African-American high school students (Silvia B. Williams) and the other on Latino students (Valverde), the striking common finding was that in both communities churchgoers had a higher graduation rate than non-churchgoers. In chapter 3, the stories of Maria and Tita will make it abundantly clear that there are important institutional presences in the lives of students who stand outside the circle of middle-class culture.

The institutions that Kareem, Maria, and Tita might depend upon, however, are not institutions that have much standing as sponsors of writing. Very seldom will college classes give students from marginalized groups a chance to write as representatives of institutions they know. And yet when it happens, the results are often crucial to the lives of the students. I remember two students I worked with at the Uni-

versity of Wisconsin who had just this sort of experience. The first was
a young African-American woman majoring in education. A professor
suggested that she write about the educational history of the women
in her family. I had worked with this student for two years through the
writing center, and I had never seen her work so hard or care so much
about how the paper was arranged and worded as she did when she
was writing and rewriting that paper. At nearly the same time, I had a
second writing center student, also an African-American woman from
an urban neighborhood, who was working on a paper about hyperten-
sion in the African-American population. She was a nursing student,
but had never showed as much investment and determination to fashion her words as she did drafting that paper.

This phenomenon is more than merely "writing about what you
know." The excitement and authorial *responsibility* these students felt
was directly related to the sponsorship they received from institutions
with which they identified. At the same time, of course, they were writing for and within other institutions that had seemed alien and hostile
to them before. But in these instances the coincident powers worked
together. This was a valuable experience for the students, and it enabled
them to feel a bit more invested in nursing and education as institutions
that could accept their experiences and histories as real. I will discuss
these two students again in the last chapter because they represent for
me one instance of a school-based solution to the problem of *double-
consciousness.* I use that term, coined first by W.E.B. Du Bois to describe
the plight of blacks who cross the "color line," to name a serious predicament for writers from marginalized communities as they struggle
to become authors.

While I was teaching at Neighborhood Academy, a school in as
dispossessed a neighborhood as the United States can produce, I was
asked by a friend to give a guest lecture in his English class at a well-
to-do private high school outside the city—I'll call it Washington Prep.
Coming from an inner-city school with holes in the floorboards and
graffiti on the outside walls, I was, of course, struck by the luxurious
grounds and buildings, but I most remember the chairs in the seminar-
type classroom. Set around a central table, these were captain's chairs,
highlighted in gold and bearing the school seal. Each student could sit
back and appear to contemplate, or lean forward and brood studiously.
Even an unkempt eighth grader drowning in his hormones could look

like an Amherst College philosophy major sitting in one of those chairs. I am not saying that out of a school like Washington Prep students could not emerge indifferent, uninspired, or even aimless writers. I am not saying that such a privileged setting cannot be the site of pain and confusion for any given kid. But students at Washington Prep would have to be deeply alienated or troubled to write as authorityless authors, not only because they know the rules of standard English, but because every student had a chance to sit in one of those chairs. Sitting there, you can think your opinions matter. Sitting there, you can imagine yourself a literary critic, a chemist, an economist. Sitting there, you can feel the sting of a teacher's comment on your paper: "Your reader will be confused by this construction!" because, by golly, you should have something to say to that reader. The most harried Washington Prep student at the bottom of the class still occupies a captain's chair, and, like a seat in the stock exchange, that chair is valuable whether the trading decisions made from it are ill advised or brilliant.

Nor do I suggest that the School District of Philadelphia go out and invest eight million dollars in captain's chairs. We could not have afforded captain's chairs at Neighborhood Academy, and they would have looked awfully silly there. We had to do it another way. The magic in captain's chairs and seminar rooms comes from their location within the magnetic field of the most powerful institutions in the land. Unfortunately, Philadelphia schools are psychically farther away from the corporate law firms, high-powered medical centers, and financial marketplaces of Center City, Philadelphia, than are the suburban schools where the children of lawyers, doctors, and business people are taught. The students of Neighborhood Academy have a deep ambivalence about leaving their neighborhoods, and they have too few bridging notions about what they will find out there if they do leave. But they do have wit and adolescent wisdom and courage, and some vague feeling that "to get a good job you need a good education." As you will see from the following chapters, students like Maria, Tita, and Kareem are frightened but willing to brave the long psychic journey into that other world.

3

Maria and Tita

Maria and Tita were new at Neighborhood Academy in 1988. Both had come from specialized public magnet schools after a year of absenteeism and failure, and both were glad to be in a smaller-scale, less-pressured environment in a school near home. Both were among the brightest and best-prepared students at Neighborhood Academy, but neither had seriously entertained college as a possibility in her future.

Maria was a seventeen-year-old senior from a Puerto Rican family. She lived with her mother, a brother, and a sister. Her father lived nearby and, although he had left the family when Maria was seven and had been living with another woman with children of her own since Maria was ten, he had remained in daily contact with Maria and her siblings and had never officially divorced Maria's mother. Maria lived within walking distance of the school in one of the poorest and most crime-ridden neighborhoods of the city. Her mother graduated from high school in Puerto Rico, and most of the extended family on both sides still lived there. Her mother did not speak English comfortably, although she had been living in Philadelphia at least since Maria was born. Maria's father had been schooled in the United States but had not finished high school; he often returned to Puerto Rico for long visits. Her brother was fifteen, had failed twice, and was expelled from Neighborhood Academy during the 1988–89 school year. Her sister was thirteen and doing very well in the school's junior high program.

Maria had left Girl's High in her junior year because she had essentially stopped going to school. Girl's High is second only to Central High School in its reputation among Philadelphia public schools for academic excellence, but Maria found it hard to get help there when she fell behind, and she felt looked down upon by her peers because of her background and home neighborhood. Whatever the reason for her perceptions, she responded to the demands at Girl's by cutting classes and letting her work slide. When she arrived at Neighborhood Academy, she presented a cheerful face and a hopeful attitude, but I came to see that she also harbored a very deep fear of failing in school.

Tita was a sixteen-year-old junior, also of Puerto Rican descent, and her family's home was only a few blocks from Maria's. She lived with her father and mother and a younger sister, but she had two older brothers as well: one stationed in Hawaii with the marines, the other serving time in prison. Only the brother in the marines and her mother had earned a high school diploma, although her sister was in one of the well-respected magnet schools in the public system and Tita often reported with some jealousy that, in the family, her sister's high grades always received more attention than Tita's. Her father was a particularly dominant figure in Tita's life because he was a strict and demanding disciplinarian, in Tita's description. He was a minister, ordained in a church program although he had never received a high school diploma, and he led a neighborhood church congregation.

Tita's history at her previous school, the prestigious Engineering and Science High School, was very similar to Maria's. Like Maria, she had felt confident and successful initially but had subsequently gotten into academic trouble. Like Maria, she remembered one previous teacher in particular—in Maria's case a math teacher, in Tita's a chemistry teacher—who ridiculed and punished her, making school life unbearable. Both had felt out of place among their peers, although they had left friends behind when they transferred to Neighborhood Academy. Both had responded to school pressures by withdrawing socially and failing academically. Both had great hope but secret fears about school. Tita differed from Maria in that she was not so outgoing; she was more introspective and less social than Maria. They became fast friends during the 1988–89 school year.

In this chapter, I will divide my discussion of Tita and Maria's writing into a section devoted to journal and interview material and a section on more formal papers written in response to classroom assignments. I will focus on Maria's schoolwork more than on Tita's because Maria was in my class throughout the academic year while Tita only joined us in January. I include Tita in the discussion, however, because I had some fascinating taped interviews with Maria and Tita together, and the two of them worked closely on a couple of large school projects relevant to this study. In short, their stories grew together that year, and those stories make a special sense when they are told together. Maria and Tita faced some common problems, and education was an important element in their strategy to solve those problems. I could not help but see how their voices intertwined by the end of the year, and their friendship itself is emblematic of the institutional allegiances from which they drew their greatest strength and about which they had their greatest fears.[1]

Maria

Here is how Maria answered the opening day questionnaire in September 1988:

---

1. Readers of this book in manuscript form have noted that in this and the following chapter I "speak for" Maria, Tita, and Kareem. One reader commented that "Professor Goldblatt plays the master ventriloquist, getting each mute aspect of the student text to speak eloquently," warning that this process presents the danger of taking over the students' voices and silencing them with my own language. Probably even more problematic, they continue, is that my narrative seems rather "effortless," as if I truly "know" what is going on in the minds of these students. To these critics I can only say: You are right, but I do not apologize. I have taken pains to quote large sections of student texts, but I cannot share the contexts without marking them with my point of view. In a larger sense, what I am trying to do in chapters 3 and 4 is to perform a teacherly reading—one that is speculative and generous as well as critical, one that constantly seeks not only what is "in" a text but also what is significant in its absence. Mary Louise Pratt's cautionary tales about "imperial eye" travelers in the Americas and elsewhere warn me to be mindful of my place in this enterprise, but I must also build relationships with the students who come into my classes. If I am to take their writing as meaningful, I must apply all that I know as I respond to their writing.

As to the charge of "effortlessness," I do not want to dismiss it with a commonplace about how hard it is to write prose that involves readers. Yes, I wish I could share more of the struggle with the reader, but I refuse to tell these stories in a turgid or specialized prose which establishes its sophistication by addressing a highly trained audience exclusively. Audience is not my only stylistic concern, either. All the problematized discourse we can muster may not get us closer to the lifestreams as they flow through classrooms and teacher-student conferences and school texts everyday, and my prose is meant to render a bit of the human— yearning, self-doubt, playfulness—in this social arrangement we call composition. I entertained the idea of disrupting the text with postmodern devices that undercut the narration, but I gave that attempt up as self-indulgent and overly literary. I am left telling the story as I've told it. I hope you will read this chapter and the next with the understanding that an academic narrator must always be in some sense as "unreliable" as Conrad's Marlowe in that most problematic of all imperial texts, *The Heart of Darkness.*

Describe something about yourself you think is distinctive or special.

I usually can tell if I'm going to get along with a person the first time I meet them. But I'm not always right. But I like to give a person a chance to prove their friendship to me before I judge them.

Describe your attitude toward writing.

I love to write. The only thing is when I'm pushed into an assignment I'm not going to like I usually do a bad job on it. But when I put both my mind and heart to it, I can usually turn in a passing paper.

Describe your best writing experience.

When I was at GHS [Girl's High School] during my sophmore year I had to write my own ending to *Of Mice and Men.* I did a rather good ending. I really liked the book and this assignment was worth doing.

Describe your worst writing experience.

My worst experience was during my junior year at GHS. My teacher wanted us to write an essay on *The Scarlet Letter.* That story was just so long and boring that when it came time to hand in the work it was not satisfactory.

What would you like to get out of English this year?

I would like to get a better understanding on certain types of literature. Instead of a teacher assigning me an assingment, I would like to pick my own topic and do research on it.

Write a short essay on your hopes and dreams for the future.

My dream for the future has always been to be a veterniary assistant. I have always been infatuated by animals. If not a vet. I would like to study wild life. Their world is so much different then ours and domesticated animals. I would like to find out how some animals can organize a group so well when they hunt. Each one has a different job to do. They seem to get along much better then humans.

This little piece touches on many of the themes of power and institutional allegiances that I find in Maria's personal and formal writing throughout the year. Before I discuss those themes, however, let me note that her writing was not particularly error-ridden or enigmatically sketchy. She made spelling errors from time to time, and she occasionally misused a preposition. In general, though, she seldom wrote fragments, handled basic capitalization and punctuation competently, and could incorporate at least simple subordinate clauses into her sentences without creating confusing statements. Tita's writing was similarly framed in standard usage and propriety. Like their outward behavior in class, their prose was correct and formally well within the boundaries of school expectations. Although both Maria and Tita wrote a more casual and slangy prose in their journals, even at moments when the story or the emotion might have taken all their attention away from the mechanics of their sentences, the grammar and diction remained by and large quite standard.

As she describes it here, the power struggle for Maria in school writing seems less with teachers than with assignments and books. She is looking for assignments she can "put both my mind and heart" into; grades or teacher expectations are not reported as compelling reasons to do well. The operant feature of the *Of Mice and Men* assignment seems to be that it puts Maria in the place of the author rather than in the more usual spot of the student reporting on the work of an author. Of course, we do not know how she felt about each teacher, but in her description of the experiences their personalities do not stand out. She seems here to focus on topics and self-initiative: "Instead of a teacher assigning me an assingment, I would like to pick my own topic and do research on it." She prefers to write in the service of an idea she perceives as her own rather than the teacher's or a famous author's.

But there is a second theme implicit here that is more central to Maria's writing. This has to do with the characteristic she identifies as significant about her—the ability to predict whether or not she's going to "get along" with someone, and her patience to wait and see about their friendship. She is a bit hazy about this claim she is making for herself. Is the characteristic friendliness or perspicacity, patience or imperiousness? Her "friendliness" is still guarded, since she says she waits for others to "prove their friendship" to her rather than actively courting new relationships. I would argue that she is primarily announcing in this questionnaire that friendship and "getting along" matter very much to her.

The assignment to end *Of Mice and Men* that Maria remembers proudly can be read then, not only as an exercise in power and control but also as a puzzle about relationships. The assignment does place the student in the author's shoes, but it also charges the student with the responsibility for having the characters literally "get along" in the story, work through their relationships to the sort of provisional resolution we expect from a novel's end. An assignment of this nature may have appealed to Maria not only for the control it offered her as an author but for the chance to shape and harmonize relationships between and among characters.

The double theme of power and relationship is particularly apparent in the description of her ambitions and dreams. Clearly she sees work in veterinary medicine as something self-directed and centered on a topic of her own choosing. But she is a bit confused about whether she wants to be a vet's assistant or the doctor in charge. This is the young woman who eventually became the editor of the school yearbook, in a school where leadership earned you little popularity among the students. Still, she was always extremely wary of the danger involved in being the one to make decisions. This essay was a fairly safe place for her to dream—although she didn't know me yet, an ambitious boast would not have been a bad way to impress a new teacher—yet the dream is to be an *assistant*.

I would not argue that there is anything wrong with Maria wanting to be a vet's assistant, but it does reveal something of her ambivalence toward ambition and education.[2] She notes in her journal soon after this questionnaire that "I'm already taking home courses in veterinary science from NCI. It's been teaching me alot about being a veterniarian assistant." She says this in the context of being "badgered by my principle about going to college" and then muses that "after I graduate I'll

---

2. Here is a good example of a place where my reading is speculative but "teacherly." Shall I simply read Maria's words as a direct message that she wants to be a veterinary assistant and go out immediately and help her find a program to train her as a technician? Perhaps I should. But, as a teacher, I have a responsibility to read in a way that will keep open my view of each student. No matter what class I am teaching, I try to be prepared for surprises and revelations, ready always to alter my vision of every student's direction. I wanted to see all of Maria's ambitions and ambivalences so that I could support her, challenge her, guide her based on her best reports about herself. There are no study guides for human beings, and no right answers to students' problems at the back of the teacher's manual. I may be wrong about a student's words as I lay out these readings, but I challenge any teacher to work with students successfully without taking the risk of active and speculative interpretation.

probably get a full time job and then later I'll probably go to college. I'm not sure what I'm going to do as of yet" (Oct. 27, 1988). I am fairly certain that at this point in the year she could not have pictured herself as being the one to tell assistants what to do.

At the same time, it seems that "veterniary assistant" can also be interchanged with "vet" in her mind, for in the third sentence of the dream essay she mentions an alternative course if she doesn't become a "vet." This is echoed by a comment she makes in her journal soon after the questionnaire: "If I can't the veterniarian that I want to be then I'd like an oppurtunity to try out different fields of work" (Sept. 29, 1988). The missing verb in the journal entry is almost as chilling as "can't"; the linguistic means of transforming herself has been omitted. Whether her speculations on other careers are a hedge against failure or merely a search for options is impossible to say, but Maria was always preparing herself for failure, as an interview I will report later makes clear. If you worry about failure, it is probably easiest to dream yourself a supporting role rather than a lead.

Her interest in animals is also an interest in human relationships, but removed from some of the trickiest parts of social interaction: "Their world is so much different then ours and domesticated animals." In this passage, she has idealized wild animals as better organized and more purposeful, capable of an unproblematic division of labor, and—recalling language she used in her opening answer—they "get along much better then humans." I assume that she means they "get along" with *each other* better, although the sentence could be asserting that animals are more likely to survive than humans because of their superior social skills. I don't know exactly what "wild animals" she is referring too, and certainly drug dealers hunting for customers or corporations for profits surpass lions in their sophisticated division of labor and singleness of purpose, but I can sympathize with her wish to find an example of animals who don't prey on each other as humans often do. At least bears don't sell poisons to each other, and I think that attracts Maria to the animal kingdom.

Maria's journal entries support her claim that animals are important to her, and they also reinforce the suspicion that animals provided for her a less complicated social world than the human one around her. She mentions two pet rabbits, three chicks, two grown dogs, three puppies, and a kitten in the course of the year. The nine entries that mention animals give us a hint of her deep attachment to her pets. Three entries link animals with important occasions for her (her birthday, the anniversary of her relationship with her boyfriend Felix, her father's return from Puerto Rico), and two portray animals acting very like simplified humans: "My puppy Rocky is really getting bad. I mean in a good way. When people come to my house he charges at their heels and bites. I just laugh" (May 30, 1989). "The kitten that I adopted on Thurs. is really getting on my nerves. She never seems to shut up. She's cute and all but I just can't wait till the day she's old enough to go with her owner" (Apr. 24, 1989). The other entries chronicle death or birth or the steady growth of a newborn. Even when she announces that her brother's fourteen-year-old girlfriend is pregnant, and she has been asked to be the godmother, her response is like that of a devoted pet owner: "Whatever [sex] it is I really don't care. I'll love it no matter what" (Oct. 5, 1988).

In response to an assignment I gave in the spring, she chose a kitten as the representative symbol of her personality—and gave quite a convincing account of herself through it. It seems that around the issue of pets she could express aggressiveness, care, grief without being caught in the complex array of emotions that families and friends provoke.

The human world, however, is the main preoccupation of her journal. The entries include stories about three deaths, a number of fights and family feuds, her boyfriend's suspension from school, two arrests, a teen runaway, and at least two of her own pregnancy scares. Maria represents the web of human relationships in entries that describe external scene as well as those that explore her feelings on a given issue or circumstance. Here, for instance, is a description of a long night on her block early in the school year:

On Tuesday there was a fight bigger than Hearst have ever saw. In about 5 hours there were 5 fights. Three of them on my block and one on third street. It was between my cousin who's 17 and some little girl about 14. The girl didn't want to fight but her mom made her. The girl got beat up by my cousin's sister-in-law Evie and by my cousin Lissette. Lissette beat the living shit our of her and sent her homing bleeding from her mouth and somewhere around her eye. Then about an hour later they came around again. This time it was the girl's cousin or something with my cousin's brother. This was really an argument but it sounded more than that. About half an hour after that the same guy came back around with two of his friends. (Sept. 22, 1988)

The solecisms that begin this passage—"have ever saw" and the fragment "Three of them . . ."—seem almost like Maria warming to the narrative task. It is only her third entry of the year, and I suspect she begins self-consciously. Should Hearst Street be identified grammatically as singular or plural? In the context of the story, Hearst certainly must have seemed plural on the night of the twentieth. And the fragment is an efficient way to tack on information about location that has little to do with the main point of the story.

Once she begins "It was between" (notice that the fight is both multiple and single), the rush of incidents is everywhere attached to this or that family network. The assertion that the fourteen year old was pushed into the fight by her mother represents the much more complex story behind the bare chronicle here, as does the sudden appearance of sister-in-law Evie to make the fight more uneven than at first. The conflict that precipitated the fight is lost in the roll call of personnel, the claims of conquest ("the girl got beat up," "Lissette beat the living shit out of her and sent her homing"—this last a pure hyperbole of the conqueror), and a few physical details ("bleeding from her mouth and somewhere around her eye"). The "they" that came around an hour after the first bout is the delegation representing the fourteen year old and presumably her bellicose mother; "and something" indicates that Maria knew her cousin's side better than the challengers. But everyone involved is there primarily because the altercation has become family business.

Time must have run out before Maria had a chance to finish her account of the fight/fights, but the theme of the story emerges nonetheless. As a reporter, Maria is at a slight remove from her own family loyalty while she tells this story. Subtly but unmistakably, she paints the fourteen year old as a victim of both her mother's vendetta and Evie and Lissette's ferocity. There is perhaps a bit of amusement and satisfaction in her note that the follow-up "fight" between the guys is more a shouting match, that the girls had the "real" fight. The ending, however, is ominous. Now that the girl's cousin and "his friends" are involved, weapons and less focused violence could make the situation explode. Yet the way she describes her cousin's victory also proclaims a certain pride in her family's strength. What Maria is forcefully representing in this entry is the importance of family ties and the connection between relationships and protection. Without a strong family, you are wickedly vulnerable at Fifth and Hearst.

Maria's journal is filled with references to family and friends. The most common topic for journal entries is the relationship with her boyfriend Felix: out of the total 116 entries, he is mentioned forty-two times. But family is a major subject also. She talks about her family in thirty-two entries. Her mother and father are mentioned twenty times each, seldom in the same entry. Her brother is mentioned seven times, usually in anger over his "freeloading" and irresponsibility. She mentions her sister only four times, usually in a playful and light tone. Felix's family is another often-mentioned topic. His mother is mentioned separately as many times as Maria's own mother, and other members of his family are mentioned an additional nineteen times. She makes mention of friends outside the two families in fourteen entries, with derogatory comments about classmates and others she knows appearing in nine entries.

These references to family and friends are not superficial. They are usually focused on the emotional, often conflicting, situations she finds herself in. Here is a representative entry about her boyfriend:

It's cold outside. I want to go home in my warm bed and go to sleep! My weekend was alright. It could have been a little better but as long as I'm with my baby everything will be fine. One thing that I wish would lower is the amount of arguing we do. It's getting really ridiculous. When we're together we can argue about 3 to 5 times a day and on the phone it could range from 1 to 3 times in a period of 6 hours. Most of the time it's over simple things and no one gets really hurt. But other times it gets really bad and I'm the one who usually gets hurt. Not physically but mentally. But he always says he's sorry but I don't accept his apology at first. I'll let him wait for an answer then I'll tell him yes I'll forgive him. I love him so much and I think that he loves me too. We have gone thru so much together. We have gone thru parents not liking either of us, affairs on both part and things like that. We are now talking over our problems (Dec. 12, 1988)

Like many of her longer entries, this one has a fascinating structure which reveals her willingness to investigate her relationships, even if she is not able to recognize the contradictions she uncovers along the way. She begins with a profession of discomfort and fatigue, a gambit for opening an entry that she used sixteen times, mostly in the first half of the year. Then Felix comes up as an antidote to what ails her, a kind of formula she uses eight times in response to troubles, especially with her family. But immediately upon invoking Felix as a talisman for well being, she turns to the problems in their relationship. She identifies arguing itself as a problem, focusing on the process rather than on any underlying conflict between them. As soon as she writes that she feels the greater victim of this process, she immediately switches to an account of how she manages Felix, then to the "us against the world" position, and finally to a hopeful conclusion that "talking over our problems" will resolve them.

From the point of view of the writer's authority, this passage presents Maria in a precarious but not powerless position. It starts with a "me against the world" posture—wishing to be safe and warm at home, withdrawn from the world. But it very soon draws Felix into the domestic circle with her, as though a love relationship better justifies her stance against the world. But, as she says in another entry, there is "trouble in paradise" (Mar. 6, 1989). Talk between Maria and Felix is not always edenic, and arguing threatens to destroy their safe retreat. She says "one thing I wish would lower is the amount of arguing we do" instead of "one thing I wish *I* would lower." This formulation of the problem doesn't put blame for arguing on either Maria or her boyfriend; the "it" that is "getting really ridiculous" is almost an entity apart from the two participants—as though arguments were like bad weather that spoils a picnic. As she continues working through the problem, the focus changes again, and she begins to see it as a matter of managing her boyfriend to make things work. She comes up with a strategy to keep from being overrun, and although she feels more hurt than Felix, she doesn't regard herself as the one to blame.

She works out a way of handling Felix, of asserting some control ("I'll let him wait for an answer") in the relationship. Her scheme sounds a bit like a plan she devised for teaching her pet rabbit Checkers not to wake her up at night: ". . . Checkers is rather active and doesn't let me sleep at night. So when I woke up this morning and found that he was still sleeping I took the oppurtunity to shake his box and show him how it feels to be awaken. I'm sure he doesn't understand what I did or my intensions but sooner or later he'll have to learn" (Sept. 27, 1990).

Although her psychology is neither strictly Skinnerian nor properly psychoanalytic, shaking the box makes emotional sense, and it probably felt satisfying to get back at the noisy rabbit. Maria may not be a good animal trainer, but she has a certain faith that if she makes her disapproval known, others will respond to her. In human relationships, you must assert that you are an agent to be reckoned with, that you are not simply there to be taken for granted. Having established her presence by making Felix wait, she forgives him. Almost like an incantation, the following sentence—"I love him so much and I think that he loves me too"—bridges her back into a stance against the world with Felix at her side, and the "talk" she puts faith in represents an effective language by which she can influence her relationship and, through her relationship, the world.

Of course the reader may be wondering at this point whether Maria really had the sort of power in her relationship that she is portraying in her journal. I don't know, although I did see Maria and Felix together a few times and saw no evidence to the contrary. However, the question is irrelevant here. Maria represents herself in her writing as a certain sort of authority, one who derives much of her power from the institutions of family and "love" relationships current in her community. Within that institutional setting, she is identified with the image of the motherly but strongly sexual young woman, someone who has a definite place in her society and someone with a right to respect and affection as well as influence over others. She represents that social reality and presents herself as a representative of that world in her journal entries. School is still a primary sponsor of the journal writing, but here the school framework allows for other, more neighborhood-based institutions to cosponsor her writing, to shine through the usual pattern of school language. Family and friends are powerful and extremely effective institutions for generating the sort of writing appropriate in a journal, and so her writing here is forceful, evocative, and rich.

A more direct connection between her sense of authority in the relationship and her faith in language is represented by her entries describing an estrangement between Felix and his mother Delores:

My vacation was alright. Sunday was about the worst day I could have had. Felix and Delores are still not speaking to each other. I tried so hard to get them to speak but to no avail. I told Felix to apologize to his mom but she tore him up like he was of no relation to her. I heard everything she said and I started to cry. I cried for him because he was to much of a man to cry. I love him so much that it hurts. I just pray that the forgive each other. (Nov. 28, 1988)

Talk, and powerful talk, is at the center of this entry. "Not speaking to each other" is Maria's phrase for the estrangement between the mother and son. She tries to establish bilateral negotiations—"to get them to speak"—and then, failing that, she urges Felix to initiate peace with a spoken apology. In the sentence "I told Felix to apologize to his mom but she tore him up like he was of no relation to her," what Felix actually says is suppressed and the words of the two women on either side of him dominate the drama. Even the crying, an outward sign of an emotional state, is a language Maria feels to be so important that she takes it on for Felix, presumably not only to express his pain but also to convey a specific message Maria thinks appropriate for Delores to see. The prayer she makes at the end of that passage is yet another type of talk Maria hopes will be powerful enough to change the state of the relationship.

The next week things are no better:

My Felix is really depressed! He keeps talking about running away and now he's just started to talk about committing suicide. He really is starting to scare me. He said that he got the idea from me. He said if I can burn myself or cut my wrists that he can do the same thing. Felix said that if he dies that his mom will be happy. I told him that she wouldn't and that what is going to happen to me. He said for me to die with him. He is going crazy.

I'm gonna have to sit him and his mom down. They have got to talk this out. (Dec. 6, 1990)

Spoken language is the medium for representing emotional states like depression, craziness, fear. This passage has at least three layers of discourse. It narrates both what Felix "keeps talking about" or "said," and also what Maria "told" him in reply. In addition, it brings into language Maria's own fears and her commentary on the situation (for example, "He really is starting to scare me;" and "He is going crazy"). She and Felix have distinct visions of the future after Felix's hypothetical suicide. Felix fears his mom "will be happy" he's dead, although it's unclear from the entry whether this is said in self-recrimination or as a criticism of his mother's love for him. Maria defends Delores and herself as real characters in Felix's melodrama. Her solution is that "they have got to talk this out," and she herself will accomplish this by making them sit down together.

In both these passages, Maria characterizes herself as powerful. She pictures herself as the one responsible for starting dialogue again. She cries for Felix when he cannot, and she speaks for Delores when he is sure she will scorn him if he dies. Her attempts at suicide ("I didn't know what I was doing," she told me when I questioned her about them) seem to have given her more authority in the field of emotional suffering, at least as far as Felix is concerned (according to her representation of Felix). The rapport Maria and Delores developed from their first conversation ("We didn't talk about anything in particular but all in all it was fun" [Oct. 20, 1988]), and visits during Delores's stay in the hospital that fall ("I pray to God every night that Delores gets better" [Nov. 10, 1988] and "I hope she gets better real soon. I miss her alot" [Nov. 14, 1988]) have put Maria in the position to mediate between the mother and son ("Whenever he starts saying these things I always get on his case. I bring up all the things she's done for him and he feels so guilty and he says that he's sorry. He'll learn" [Nov. 10, 1988]). She has taken up a strong position in the family, at least as she relates it in the journal.

But, of course, this is a power with definite limits, a power grounded in the specific context of her community's institutions. The roles Maria plays which allow her power, as chronicled again and again in the journal, are roles within a complex family environment or a neighborhood social structure she knows intimately. What power Maria exercises within families depends upon her ability to gauge relationships between other family members—especially between son and mother, both for Felix and Delores and for Maria's brother and her mother. Outside the home, her power depends both on how tough she can appear to those who might intimidate her, and how well she is able to read a situation and tell what the safe limits are. In a few cases, she threatens to beat up girls who might give her trouble, and she reports dreams of fighting even though she says, "I don't know why I'm having these kinds of dream because I'm not a violent person at all" (Dec. 14, 1988). But her fighting—in dream or reality—is mostly symbolic, used to stake out territory and express the tensions in close community ties. Her standing among her peers derives primarily from her savvy about the prerogatives and limits of roles in the social order around her.

In a fascinating and, for this study, quite relevant juxtaposition, Maria links her fears about speaking in public to a contemplation of friends in her life:

> Well, I've got to do my music report today. I'm not really up to it. I'm not good in front of people. My hands get red and they start to shake. After my reports, it usually takes me awhile before my heartbeat gets back to normal. I hate oral reports. Well its not actually oral because all I really have to do is hand out my copies and play the music. Any which way I'll be up in front of the class in front of people I've just met this year. I'm still not comfortable with these people. And I never quite will be since I'll be graduating this year. But as for the friends I've made, I hope that we'll stay that way for a long time. Friends are what makes a person what they are. Without friends you are left with an empty space within yourself. You can have everything but without friends to share it with you have nothing. (Oct. 13, 1988)

The efficacy of her speech, the influence she may have had on an audience—whether composed of a lone buddy or a class of kids—depends, in her formulation, largely on the extent to which she is "comfortable" with her listeners. In a statement whose number agreement is simultaneously confusing and eloquent, she says, "Friends are what makes a person what they are." Is a person a singular entity influenced by the single collective noun "friends"? Do friends make you what you—in your single self—are, or do they make you what *they* are? The more I read Maria's journals, the more convinced I am that for her the idea that authority might be a purely personal or psychological quality is nonsense, even though Maria was a very distinct personality in the school, a leader who could speak her mind. When she spoke with authority, to her boyfriend, to her family, to her classmates, to her teacher, she was always speaking out of a strong sense of the network that surrounded her and gave her an identity even when it caused her pain. Friends and family made her voice what it was.

Tita

Although Tita was younger than Maria, she seemed on first impression to be more mature, probably because she was more somber than Maria. She laughed easily and could chatter in the mornings or lunch over potato chips and sodas like the rest of her friends, but in conversation and class discussion she tended to be more thoughtful and serious. I knew her through the first half of the year merely as Maria's friend, but when two students left my English class at the end of first semester, her English teacher and the principal suggested I ask Tita to join us. She agreed without hesitation, saying that she wanted a new challenge. Within a few days she was participating in our discussions and turning in some of the best work in the class. She had known the other students in our group because they were all in her other classes, but the reputation of our class must have been a bit daunting. Her year at Engineering and Science, however, probably helped her in the transition—despite the ultimate outcome of that public school experience—because she knew we couldn't throw anything at her harder than she had seen at her previous school. She started the second semester with admirable self-confidence and hope, at least on the surface.

The ninety-nine total entries in her journal of 1988–89 present a kid with far greater tensions at home and in the neighborhood than Maria faced, and they suggest that what looked like greater maturity may have been sadness and patience born of pain. Like many students at Neighborhood Academy, the school hours were probably some of the safest and calmest times in Tita's week. In the early fall, she wrote seven entries about violence in the street outside her house. Some of the violence was not aimed directly at her family. Note that,when compared to Maria's comparable entry above (Sept. 27, 1988), Tita's description is more graphic and the violence more uncontained:

Last night there was a big street fight around my way. A bunch
of people had guns, bats and poles. Everybody was hitting on each
other, without knowing why. My neighbors said that it all started
when a gang with weapons came running down breslow, and
when they got to Bright (my street) they stopped and started
fighting with the guys on the corner. Someone called the police,
but by that time most of the fighting was over and the gang had
departed. The cops always come too late. (Sept. 26, 1988)

But other entries portray more focused threats:

This was a pretty bad weekend. This guy on the corner around
my house keeps trying to threaten my family. He thinks he so bad.
He stares at us and says disgusting things to us. My father doesn't
believe in violence so he doesn't do anything. I'm scared to walk
home today because he said that he would be waiting for me at
2:00. If he touches me I'm going to beat the shit out of him. If
he knew that I have 2 older brothers he would leave me the hell
alone. He is a coward. My mother told me that she is going to
talk to "Fatboy" (his boss) and tell him that if he doesn't get rid
of him that she's going to call the cops and tell them everything
she knows. We have lived in this neighborhood for 13 years and
its not fair that we leave just because some jackass thinks he can
do what ever he does. (Oct. 17, 1988)

As in the world Maria represents, safety for Tita depends upon
family strength and knowing the neighbors. The unnamed character
who threatens them here probably does know that Tita has two older
brothers—and he knows too that both of them are far away. But Tita's
mother is willing to go over his head and talk to the boss of the operation. She is not afraid to speak to a drug dealer because she knows
how the system works, and she knows that its corporate hierarchy is
vulnerable to pressure. As with Maria's writing, Tita's entries also portray language as powerful: the threats come in the form of "disgusting
things" the man says, the mother's response will be "to talk to 'Fatboy.' " Yet here we can see that language both gains power by its proximity to violence and also serves as a buffer between and among people;
when language breaks down, then the situation devolves into a chaos
where "Everyone was hitting on each other, without knowing why."

Tita's entries do sometimes suggest that the outside violence draws the family closer within their domestic circle:

Last night someone was trying to freak my family. They were making loud noises and banging things in our back yard. My mom and me were scared stiff. Finally my father went outside to check around (my sister slept through the whole things) When we came upstairs, my mom stayed with me and got into my bed. We talked about a half an hour and we laughed the other half. Then I fell asleep. At 3 oclock in the morning, the noises started again, this time it sounded like someone was trying to break in. Again everyone (except my sister) was awake and my father went to check again. In a way it was sort of fun, because I got to talk and laugh with my mom. It seems like we always talk more and laugh more when something's wrong. I think it strengthens our relationship a whole lot. When we talk like that it feels like she's my older sister or my best friend, instead of my mom. I like spending time with mom like this. It cheers me up. (Oct. 20, 1988)

Touching moments like this, however, are far outweighed in her journal by the tensions within the family. Tita writes even more often than Maria about her family (forty-seven compared to thirty-one entries). Where Maria writes nine entries that can be described as critical of family members—and most are relatively mild complaints about the lack of "independence" from her family or the privileged treatment her brother receives from her mother—Tita writes nineteen anguished entries about her home life. There are at least four or five other entries where the language is pained but unspecific, and a number of blank entries marked only by dates (my total of ninety-nine entries does not include blanks). From conversations with Maria during times when Tita refused to talk to anyone about problems that were obviously troubling her, I can be pretty certain that most of her silences and vague references involved her family. For her mother, sister, and father, there are almost as many negative or angry comments as there are positive or neutral ones. She is only consistently affectionate and hopeful about her two older brothers. She is constantly counting the time until they return home, as if they will bring with them a happier and more tranquil domestic life.

Her most furious and frightening entries are about her father, who is presented as insensitive to her in church gatherings—often embarrassing her in front of congregants—and uncommunicative and even brutal in private. Perhaps her most frank entry is this one:

> My father got on my nerves yesterday afternoon. He and I have never really had a good relationship, but he's still my father, and he should give me some space. We have never seen eye to eye. Sometimes I think he hates me, sometimes I hate him very much. He has tried to hit me a couple times and he has hit me a few times. Sometimes I feel like killing him. I'm scared that some day I will kill him. Once I kept a knife next to my bed, thats how scared I was. He makes me hurt inside. I wish that he could love me just a little. I can't really say that I love him. (Jan. 5, 1989)

In short, Tita's journal represents the writer as a person besieged both from without and within her home. Although she has some entries in which she talks about her father in a more neutral fashion, as when she reports something he did along with the family, there is little truly positive about him. She represents herself as respecting and fearing him and little else. Moreover, though her words are sometimes kinder about her mother, she ends an entry the day before she wrote the above passage with the sentences: "I'm not sure if its because I don't understand my family or my family doesn't understand me. I find it hard to find encouragement at home" (Jan. 4, 1989). I'm sure many adolescent journals have passages such as this, but taking her journal entries and interview material altogether, I cannot help but feel the strength implicit in the balance and understatement of those two simple sentences.

In a different way than Maria, Tita draws strength from her friends and her school. Maria's mainstay is the social position and support given her by her boyfriend and his family, but she also mentions other friends fourteen times in her journal. Tita mentions no present steady boyfriend, but she devotes twenty-two entries to male and female friends she feels close to. Given her home and neighborhood situation, the closing entry of her journal stands out from the usual high school sentiments at the end of a school year:

> Well! school is almost over! This year has been an experience. My life has changed so much and its because I came here. I'm actually

doing work, just a year ago I wouldn't open a book! I think my overall attitude has changed. I turned from a mean annoying brat into a calmer friendlier person. This is going to be a sad end of the year for me. I'm going to lose some people who I love very much. Hopefully next year I can find the loving relationships that I found this year. My feelings right now are mixed. I'm happy because my friends will start a new begining of education; and I'm sad because I know that I will never find friends as good as them.

Neighborhood Academy worked its magic on angry and confused adolescents largely by providing a place where they could feel part of a supportive circle of friends, and clearly the above passage is a tribute to that school environment. But Tita's authority as a writer probably derives at least in part from her perception that school and schooling offer her sponsorship for a positive formation of self, for a sense of herself as an author with ideas and feelings to express. Journal writing must have provided a sort of "room of one's own" within which Tita could "realize" her feelings and give them institutional reality through written language. In a final questionnaire that Tita wrote for me, her answers juxtapose an intense relief at having found a school that would encourage her with a real enthusiasm for writing:

Do you feel like you have good models in your life for reading and writing? In other words, have you known people who value reading and writing?
I've never really known someone who really values reading and writing. The first person who really told me to put my feelings, my ideas and my thoughts onto paper was Mr. L [her English teacher at Neighborhood Academy during the first semester of 1988–89]. Noone in my family has ever pushed me to express my opinions.

Have you had much support among family and friends to do well in school?
Noone has ever helped me out in school. I feel like I've been doing it all alone. My parents tell me to get good grades but that's about it. If I get bad grades they put me down and punish me but they don't encourage me to do better. They expect a lot of me but they don't help me out. I think thats why I did so bad at E and S. I'd get bad grades and they'd threaten me in one way or

another. Now I have all my teachers at Neighborhood. There I know that the teachers will help me out. I haven't had that before.

What do you think you've learned about writing this year? Do you feel like you have more control over writing now than before? Do you feel you have something to say to people?
I've learned that writing is one of the best ways to have your feelings, opinions or thoughts heard. I feel like I do have more control over writing. I think that now I enjoy writing more too. I think that I have lots of things to say to people. I feel like I should be able to express my own opinions. It feels great when other people read my writing and like it.

Certainly the fact that she frames her answer about writing in social terms reflects, to some extent, my own bent in teaching writing. But social terms were so crucial to Tita, for she failed in school before—in my opinion—largely because she felt she did not belong in the social system the school offered her and there was little support at home. As we shall see when we turn to the interview material, family and neighborhood provide an all-encompassing network for Maria and Tita within which they know their place and can function. Even in the case of the harsh conditions Tita faced, she could not imagine stepping out of her environment. Tita was so much more successful at Neighborhood Academy because she found not only a way to exercise authority based on her familiarity with friends and neighbors but also she was sponsored by an institution that credited her with personal worth. Not that the academic content of her classes was neighborhood-based (in my class we studied Irving, Hawthorne, Poe, and Douglass for example), but her classmates were people who would not look down on her because of her background, and her teachers were sensitive to what was familiar and unfamiliar in the material they covered in class. Maria got a bit more support than Tita from other areas of her life, but she also needed school sponsorship. What they feared about college was that they would lose everything by entering an alien environment.

Interviews

In one interview with Tita and Maria, they talked with me extensively about why it was frightening to go to college. Maria had recently been accepted to a small Catholic women's college in the area, but she was quite hesitant to go there. I had a strong feeling that their success at Neighborhood Academy, and the authority with which they wrote their eloquent journal entries, were directly related to the school's placement within the fabric of the network they knew. College represented a radical shift away from the neighborhoods, and so I was particularly interested in how they felt about that change:

> *Tita*: My mom wants to leave our neighborhood because you know its a bad neighborhood, in the summer especially the shooting. And in my neighborhood, the corner is a big selling corner for the drug pushers. And she wants to leave, she just wants to leave the house and everything. But I don't want to leave that neighborhood because I know what that neighborhood's all about and I'm cool with them, I don't have any problems with anybody and I know how to survive there, you know. I can get around those obstacles and I think that if I go to another place, then I'm not going to know what's going to be up there. I don't know. I feel safe in my neighborhood even though it's bad.
>
> *EG*: You feel safe even though you could get shot?
>
> *Tita*: If we were to move, and I don't know how I would survive with the different people. I know how to survive with these drug pushers because you know I don't have any problems with them, and they don't have any problems with me. I don't try to get with them or nothing, it's just that I know how to survive in my block. But if I were to leave I just think I couldn't make it somewhere else. It's real bad, and the shooting and everything, but there's something in my mind that says I couldn't leave—it's like I love that place there, even though it's so bad. 'Cause it's my home.
>
> *EG*: What do you love about it?
>
> *Tita*: 'Cause I grew up there, that's all I know. That's where I was brought up. All those people, although some of them went through the wrong roads or whatever, I know them and I know what all those people are about. That's the way I grew up and that's my place and if I left—psst—I can't hack it.
>
> *EG*: Do you feel like you can predict what they're going to do in situations?
>
> *Tita*: Yeah.
>
> *EG*: And maybe it's hard to predict other people?

Tita: Um hum, because I already know them. They been with me—most of the people on the corner I grew up with them—most of the guys I know them. We went to school together and stuff like that, and I know what they're all about. I know how they think. But if I go somewhere else I'm not going to really know what those people are like.

EG: And how they think?

Tita: Yeah.

EG: Is that important to know how people think?

Tita: Yeah! In this neighborhood it is. Because if you don't, you don't know them at all.

EG: Then you could get shot, right. Or firebombed or . . .

Tita: Yeah, you could. Your house could get burned down, or your car. And I don't have no problems in my neighborhood.

My attentive readers will notice that in fact Tita has described in her journals some fairly sizable problems in her neighborhood. Her assertion here that she has "no problems" is not, however, pure public relations. For her, safety in the neighborhood is based on an insider's knowledge. She understands the shaping experiences of the people around her who might threaten her. She feels certain she knows what they are thinking and when they will act in a way hurtful to her and her family, and she feels certain that that knowledge will help her decide when to get off the streets and when to meet threats with counter-threats.

The safety her knowledge provides is a product of the local economy of power. She tacitly agrees to give up some control over her life—a night here and there hiding from a gun battle, a longer walk home to avoid a bad corner at a certain time of day—for the sake of being able to live relatively unmolested within her sphere. Tita gives a particularly stark example of this economy when she talks about a phone conversation she had with a friend from Engineering and Science High School who lived in a quieter part of town:

Tita: She asked me, "Well, what about these people? Are you around them and what not?" And I'm like: in my neighborhood the biggest drug pushers are my next door neighbors, and they have a beautiful house that they did from top to bottom—new, completely new. It's a beautiful house, and they are drug pushers. And she goes, "Well, aren't you scared that your phone might be tapped?" Now I know for a fact that my phone is tapped, and they have the tap next door.

EG: Who tapped it? Oh, the drug dealers have a tap on your phone?

Tita: Yeah, 'cause my father's a minister, and they're scared that my father might call the cops, even though the cops don't ever show up. But I know for a fact that my phone is tapped. And so I go, "I know my phone is tapped. I know they're listening." And she goes "Aren't you scared?" "No. I'm not saying anything about them—why should I be scared?" OK? I don't have any problem with them as long as I don't do anything to them. It's just you feel safe even though it's a bad area and it's a bad—it's a problem, but you're safe in that problem for some reason.

Again, language enters as a powerful force. Tita can even tell her friend about the tap and not be saying the dangerous words that might bring retribution down on her head. "You're safe in that problem" because as long as you concede the power to speak aloud you are permitted to elaborate on the delusion—you may even describe it to your uninitiated friends—that there is no problem.

Language, knowledge, power: these are all elements of an institution. In her journal entries and her response to questions, Tita is outlining the institutions that dominate and shape her life. Yet the economics of the street and the domestic arrangements she understands clash with the values and inquiries fostered by her school, which remains a primary sponsor for journal writing and other class assignments. Thus, whatever authority Tita develops as a school writer must come in direct conflict with the power relationships she accepts in her neighborhood and home. She can write to me that "I think that I have lots of things to say to people. I think that I should be able to express my opinions." Yet, the opinions she must maintain for safety's sake at home are that the shooting outside her house is not particularly dangerous to her and that her knowledge of her neighbors protects her from harm. Her school self might disagree with that assessment, but her home self cannot afford to question or revise those beliefs. When we combine the neighborhood economy with the power arrangements within her home, we can picture a young woman whose intellectual growth and personal sense of power as an author within the world of school must collide eventually with all she knows about self-preservation.

Maria's response to the question of leaving raises other questions. She, too, stresses the need for intimate knowledge to survive in the neighborhood: "They don't bother me. I don't bother them. They just stand there, but if I move somewhere else I'd be looking like 'who's that?' And I wouldn't know them. And you know you don't know when they're going to start shooting or anything." But, unlike Tita, Maria focuses on what moving might do to her own sense of self:

> When moving from one block to another I had a lot of hard times because the people that I would meet I would like to impress them, and I wouldn't act like myself, and I would act like they wanted me to act. And I feel that's the same way I'm going to do when I go to college and you know I'm not going to feel right and I'm going to feel guilty because I'm lying to them and I'm lying to myself 'cause I'm not telling them who I really am.

Tita takes this psychological idea of losing who you "really" are in a new environment and turns it once again into an issue of social knowledge:

> *Tita*: In your block you can be yourself.
> *Maria*: Right.
> *Tita*: 'Cause everybody knows. They know what you're about and you know what they're about. 'Cause somewhere else with different people, they don't know anything, really anything about you—what's your background like and you just try to act like another person. You're not yourself, and you're not comfortable, you know, around them.

However, Maria is less concerned about how comfortable she will be socially than she is about how well she can perform individually in an environment without her network:

> *EG*: So is that one of the big things that's keeping you from going to college [not feeling comfortable around others]?
> *Maria*: No.

EG: It's not. So you think you could put up with that?

Maria: I could put up with that. But one thing—when I came out of my elementary school and went into Girl's High I felt really stupid. And I'm afraid the same thing's gonna happen in college.

EG: Oh. That's interesting. You never told me that before. So you're worried it's going to be the same kind of experience it was at Girl's High? That makes sense.

Maria: And failing. If I go, and fail, I don't think I could take it.

For Maria, failure—and the humiliation it would bring—is the great looming danger. Maria is much more certain of the danger in college than Tita is. She is less concerned about what others will do to her, but more concerned that she will be unable to do the job:

EG: Like the people aren't carrying guns or knives in college, but they have a different kind of power.

Maria: It's just myself—that I can't—handle the work. That's what I'm afraid of—of me failing and being stupid to them. That's scary.

Perhaps failure is a devastating prospect not only because of what it may make her feel about herself alone, but what it could imply about her whole social group. If she is judged and found wanting, the judgment not only applies to her individual skills but also to everything she was taught, everyone who raised her and shaped her. Since, as both girls say, their neighborhood is "what they know," a poor showing in school suggests that the defining institutions of their lives don't measure up to institutions that already lord over them in terms of wealth and prestige.

To a significant degree, then, future school success becomes for Maria and Tita a struggle between different institutions for their allegiances, if not for their souls. They are profoundly afraid that college, and particularly the other students they meet there, will try to "change" them into people who despise their origins:

EG: Are you scared about yourself changing?

Tita: Yeah. I don't want to be something that I'm not. And I don't want to change for somebody else, and I'm scared that if

I'm caught under them—if they catch me—that I'm going to turn
into one of them, and I want to be my own person.

EG: Now what does "turning into one of them" mean?

Tita: It means something's wrong. Maybe an example would
be regretting who I am, or regretting where I came from, my
background—regretting that I came from that neighborhood.

Maria: There was an article that Mr. Walsh had gave us about
an Hispanic. He went to school and everybody in his neighborhood pushed him to be white, and now that he's thirty or forty
or something he regrets it, and he knows very little Spanish, and
now he's trying to become Hispanic again and it's hard and he
regrets it.

Tita: I live in my neighborhood and I know it's so bad but I
have never my whole life regretted that I live there 'cause that was
chosen for me and I was put there, and I have never regretted it.

Tita and Maria feel safe, even with all the dangers of their neighborhood and home life, yet they both want to engage more with the
outer world that holds other possibilities for them. Maria wrote in a
journal entry addressed to me, during the time when all her teachers
were urging her to go to college directly after graduation: "Going to
college is my dream and someday I am going to fulfill that dream. Some
day, hopefully it'll be soon. I do want to better myself. Just give me
some time and space." Tita, who as a junior felt less direct pressure to
make a decision about college, said in her closing questionnaire response that "now I feel more confident in myself and I know that I can
be something if I just work hard for it." The contradiction implicit in
both their statements is that their very words contain an unconscious
concession that Maria can only "better" herself by leaving her neighborhood, and Tita cannot be "something" now because she must
"work hard" to attain that distinction. These are contradictions all of
us face when we accept the project of moving up in the social hierarchy
of our culture, but for Maria and Tita the hazards of the leap into
another economic class are particularly harsh and unforgiving. I do not
say the leap is not worth the risk for them and their families, but I
would be dishonest to say that there is no real risk for them. Others
have tried the waters and found them just as rough as Maria and Tita
think they will be.

Maria Writes About Her Neighborhood

Maria wrote many sorts of essays and brief comments in my class through the 1988–89 school year. For the sake of continuity, and because the revision changes were so extensive, I will concentrate in this section on the two drafts of the neighborhood description paper that Maria wrote. In the next chapter, I will discuss drafts that Kareem wrote in response to the same assignment. Tita did not write a neighborhood paper since she was not in the class for the assignment, but I will conclude this section with a brief discussion of projects both Maria and Tita worked on. These projects were not traditional writing assignments, but they were designed to foster the development of authority in student writers, and their results were quite exciting.

Soon after the first semester began, Maria turned in the following draft of a paper describing her neighborhood:

September 16, 1988

My Neighborhood

My neighborhood is a typical one. The houses around here were not very well kept, but now many people are now taking pride in their homes. Many houses this summer gave their homes either a new paint job or added a new porch to the front of their house. Many people. Many people added those lights to their homes. At night I like to sit on my steps and just think. It's rather quiet here at night.

As for the people on this block, we've got all kinds. There are people whom I've known for years whom I get along with very well. Then there are those whom you just can't get along with. They swear that they are better than you. And I don't appreciate that. I know that everyone is unique but no one is better than anyone else. Then their are those who like to cause trouble. They're alot of talk but no action. Then there are those whom you're not really friends or enemies with. You just say hi to them when you see them.

As for the drug scene, I've had my share of it. I've never taken it but I know those who deal in it. The major corner around here is 5th and Norris. Some of my friends work there and they make alot of money on it. But still don't think it's right. The things are so bad around there that on some occasions when I'm just waiting for the bus people come up to me asking if I'll sell them drugs. I just look at them and send them up the street.

So this is my neighborhood. It's not the best but I can live with it.

This essay is neatly divided into three simple topics: the overall appearance of the neighborhood, the people on the block, and the drug scene. Perhaps its major claim is the one it begins with—that her neighborhood is "typical"—and it makes an even vaguer secondary claim in the conclusion that the neighborhood is "not the best but I can live with it." It has very few mechanical errors, and most indicate nervousness rather than confusion over standard usage. For instance, she makes a copying error in paragraph one ("Many people.") and later misuses "their" in paragraph two, amid correct uses for each of the homonym forms in the rest of the paper. Her almost obtrusively correct use of "whom" in paragraph two says more about the good manners she is attempting to display than it does about the people we might find on her block.

In short, this is the familiar high-school/college freshman paper that exhibits correct form and says practically nothing. Yet the absence of a consciously developed main point, and its silence about the central issues we have already seen Maria discuss in her journal, make this first draft peculiarly eloquent. Lest we are tempted to excuse her because it's still too early in the year to expect vivid writing, I suggest my reader glance back at Maria's description of the fight on her block, a journal entry dated four days after this assignment. The grammar isn't as good, and there isn't a single "whom," but the account is far more engaging.

Let me begin a close consideration of this draft by contemplating the key word of the first sentence—"typical." As we will see, Kareem uses this leveling approach in the first draft of his neighborhood paper as well, but Maria may be using the term more innocently here. First of all, Maria probably had traveled less around the city than Kareem. Most parents in her neighborhood are extremely protective of their children and keep them close to home. Maria does not write in her journal, as Kareem does, about shopping trips downtown, nor for that matter does she reveal any expertise about the bus system, the way Kareem does. Neighborhood Academy was in her neighborhood, so she didn't have to travel through other areas to get there. Girl's High, her previous school, was in a busy location several subway stops up Broad Street from Maria's neighborhood, but she would never have had to pass through other residential areas on the way to or from school. She does mention a trip to Lancaster, Pennsylvania, in her journal, but that was after this draft was completed. Of course, she had visited Puerto Rico a few times, but she probably wouldn't consider the island communities she knows examples of "typical" American neighborhoods.

Thus, Maria may really have had such limited experience that she thought her neighborhood was typical. She may also be saying "neighborhood" but meaning block, for she focuses on "the people on this block" in the second paragraph. If that were the case, she might be comparing her block to others in the Puerto Rican neighborhood; she might be roughly accurate to say her block is typical of others around her.

The point of naming her neighborhood "typical," however, involves more than a mere comparison. What Maria is asserting here is not so much typicality as normality. Maria makes the valid point that the people in her neighborhood live like the people in every city neighborhood. They want to improve their property values. Some people get along better with their neighbors while others hold themselves aloof. The drug trade threatens everyone, but many resist. The lack of development in the account is an argument for Maria's neighborhood being, in general, like other high school students' neighborhoods. Nothing special, nothing different.

Being different can make one frighteningly vulnerable. Maria and Tita may not know much about other neighborhoods, but both had experiences in schools where they felt other students thought their neighborhoods superior to the Puerto Rican neighborhood, and Maria and Tita felt shut out by the attitudes they perceived. The significance of this difference came out in the May interview discussed above when I asked Tita what seemed unsafe about going to college:

> *EG*: Do you think people would beat you up or shoot you?
> *Tita*: Well I would feel sort of like left out and apart from everybody else. I would feel different. That's what it is—everybody else would be different from me.
> *EG*: Uh-uh. And that feels unprotected?
> *Tita*: Yeah.

So in Maria's first rendering of her neighborhood, it is important for her to represent a community devoid of its characteristic details: street vendors with signs in Spanish, beautiful gardens behind impassable fences, burnt-out rowhouses, vacant lots, and potholes in the street so deep you could fill them with water for wading pools in the summertime. She wants to present her readers with a community life that is regular and unremarkable, for anything else might open herself up for ridicule or scorn.

The first paragraph, however, contains traces of other stories to tell. The shift in tense and the repetition of "now" in the second sentence presses the idea that the neighborhood is changing, on its way up. Although the visual focus is on how the houses look, the dramatic interest of the paragraph revolves around the "many people" who are trying conscientiously to take hold of their neighborhood. She has a bit of trouble balancing what the reader sees in the neighborhood with what the reader should know about the people behind the scenes doing the work. She makes the mistake of claiming the houses themselves did the home improvements, but she may also be identifying the people in the houses with the word "house," as when members of a sorority or fraternity are referred to as "the house." When you think of your block, people are associated with the houses and vice-versa, and Maria wants to represent her neighbors and their homes in the best light she can.

The transcription error "Many people." indicates how much her mind is on human agency here. The following sentence, "Many people added those lights to their homes," emphasizes what the homeowners did while leaving the object vague; readers cannot know what the phrase "those lights" refers to. Student writers often forget that local references don't carry over to nonlocal readers, but her concern here is not to describe the new kind of lights anyway. She wants us to understand that they are yet another example of the changes announced by the double "now" of the second sentence. To reinforce her point that the neighborhood is becoming more livable, she introduces an apparent nonsequitur in the final two sentences of the paragraph. The quality of life on her street is quite respectable, despite what others might think: Hearst Street is quiet enough at night for a person to sit on her front steps and think.

This first paragraph, then, holds within it certain strong and particular claims about Maria's neighborhood that go well beyond her assertion that it is typical. She claims that people are beginning to take more pride in the appearance of their homes, she claims the homes have some new outward signs of that pride, and she claims that her block is a quiet place for contemplation of an evening. Moreover, she is representing her neighbors as hardworking, concerned, and competent. She does not actually say whether her neighbors own their own homes, but she implies that they do, with all the repairs and improvements she points out. This first paragraph not only represents a "typical" and industrious neighborhood, but it also presents the author as a representative of a community for which she feels pride and affection.

The paragraph about the people on the block is more problematic. She wants to package local human relations into a neat, four-part array of people:

1. Those "I get along with very well"
2. Those "you can't get along with"
3. Those "who like to cause trouble"
4. Those "you're not really enemies or friends with"

Everyone can fall into one of those categories, and no reader can fault Maria for being either overly judgmental or incomplete in her categories. We are not given the relative numbers in each category, nor are we told what overall conclusion she draws from this survey. From the concluding category we might assume she combines numbers 2 and 3 into one set of "enemies." If we take a sentence count as representative, we could conclude that her enemies far outnumber her friends and acquaintances. Not counting the topic sentence, which is mostly a refrain of the "typical" theme (every block will have "all kinds" on it), there are eight sentences devoted to neighbors. Only one is concerned with friends, six are concerned with enemies, and two with the unaligned. Clearly there are stories here, particularly of the negative variety, ready to burst forth, but they are reined in by a structure designed to represent the neighborhood as "typical."

The shift in references from "we" and "I" to "you" is significant here. In the opening sentence, Maria is representing herself as belonging to the community with the first-person-plural pronoun. In the second sentence, she must use "I," even if some teacher in her past has told her it isn't allowed, because neither "you" nor "one" will have known these people for years. The rest of the paragraph is addressed to "you," almost as if she is trying to get the reader personally incensed at her enemies ("They swear that they are better than you") or to confront her neighbors directly ("You just say hi to them when you see them").

Although the effect is a little comic, the pronouns do work to generalize these relationships rather than hang them all on Maria's individual experience. She appears hesitant to categorize the people on her block exclusively on the basis of her personal view, even though that is essentially all she has to report. Instead, the language reaches to establish principles for classifying people that will work in other neighborhoods as well. Again, Maria emphasizes similarities and likenesses lest the reader judge her as different and thus beneath concern. Yet in order to realize her portraits fully, to bring to life the complex relationships hemmed in by her abstract categories, she must choose to explore the first-person rhetorical position with which she begins the paragraph and risk revealing her investment in the neighborhood life.

We get a glimpse of a more powerful first-person narrative in the next paragraph. Drugs are the most rhetorically challenging topic in the paper for an author attempting to represent her neighborhood as typical. Maria knows that people come from all over the Philadelphia area to buy drugs at Fifth and Norris. She also knows that drug organizations employ young people in her neighborhood the way factories and warehouses used to in the old days. The best she can do is to normalize it in her prose, accept its reality but register her objection to it. The topic sentence confronts the issue directly and, to my ear, courageously: "I've had my share of it." Here she represents herself as personally involved, as though she is standing up to would-be accusers and saying: "Yes, if you want to reject my neighborhood for its drug-dealing, you'll have to reject me, too. I don't like it, but I'm not going to deny how much it is a part of my world." The entire paragraph uses only "I" as the nominative pronoun, never "you." She solves the rhetorical problem by assuming the first-person narrative she would not accept in the previous paragraph.

Maria normalizes the subject of drugs by dividing it into two parts and dealing with the more defensible part. The second sentence asserts she's "never taken it," but she knows "those who deal in it." The users and the sellers are the two sides of the economy on the street. Beyond the denial that she has ever used "it" personally, the only time we glimpse drug use in this paragraph again is when "people" approach her, mistaking her for a seller. She dismisses "them" with a look, and directs "them" up the street. But the selling end of "it" is adopted in this paragraph as an unfortunate economic fact of life, more a symptom of how bad things have gotten than a particular sin in itself.

The revealing pronoun in this paragraph is "it." The referent is identified only twice, first in the opening phrase and later in the clause, "if I'll sell them drugs" (presumably that if-clause is a paraphrase of other people's words and, combined with the following "I just look at them and send them up the street," the expression "sell them drugs" is inflected with distaste and disdain). The five intervening instances of "it" stand not only for the literal crack vials and baggies, but for the whole wracked world of addiction and the desperation it generates. She boxes away that intractable reality into the pronoun and concentrates here on the one fact that both keeps the business running and assimilates it into American institutions: "they make alot of money on it." She cannot see her friends and relations in the drug trade as devils or death-dealers. As much as she may despise what the trade is doing to her neighborhood, she cannot afford to cast away a significant portion of her community network. I know that Maria worked terribly hard to get her boyfriend out of the business, but she could not have sustained that struggle if she had merely written "drugs" off as an evil empire to reject out of hand. The "it" in this paragraph stands for a dirty business, and the pronoun puts her at one remove from contamination, much as mechanical arms protect uranium workers from radioactivity. Even discussing the subject is risky business, but "it" is so much a feature of her world that she must represent drugs somehow in her written language.

"There" is another pivotal word in this paragraph. It literally refers to the corner of Fifth and Norris, but it also serves to institutionalize that corner as an identifiable place of business and community. To outsiders, Fifth and Norris might seem like yet another bustling but broken-down city intersection, with more than the average number of men hanging around, some sitting and talking to their friends, others waving casually at passersby, a few doing a strange sort of speeded-up dance on the sidewalk and even into the street. Maria's phrase "Some of my friends work there" makes it clear that this is a place of business, institutionally not unlike a food store or a welfare office. The workers show up for their shifts and fulfill a prescribed job description, their supervisors check up on them now and then, and they expect compensation in accordance with industry standards.

Her later phrase, "things are so bad around there," refers to Fifth and Norris not as a retail outlet but a neighborhood locus, a place where people have to carry on the regular affairs of their lives. This "there" refers to the larger institution upon which the drug trade is superimposed, and the drama of the interaction between the two neighborhood institutions has all the elements of classic tragedy. Maria's honest and unadorned treatment of the scene could serve well as choral commentary on tragic action. It is as if when she "sends them up the street" she is ushering characters onto center stage and furthering the plot.

The peculiarly defective sentence "But still don't think it's right" could easily draw a "Subj?" notation in the margin from the earnest writing teacher. Perhaps she just miscopied again, as she did with the "Many people." above. But this defect is eloquent, for it speaks to the moral haze surrounding the issue. Parents, siblings, friends, even some drug dealers themselves might occupy the place of subject for that sentence; everyone thinks "it's not right," but no one knows what that opinion should mean. Are the drugs wrong, or the economic situation that fosters the drugs? How wrong is it? Who is implicated in its wrongness? Should stores or private schools refuse payments when they come in wads of ones, fives, and tens? Should Mama let the phone service go because otherwise Junior is going to pay for it with money he earned at Fifth and Norris? To decide what the subject of that sentence should be is indeed to be an "authority" on the issue at hand, for the community authorizes Maria's writing far more than the learned establishments of criminal justice, sociology, or political science.

When Maria comes to conclude her brief argument for the neighborhood's typicality, she is hard put to say very much. She has managed to represent the neighborhood without being overwhelmed by the human stories, in all their fullness and contradiction, that her neat rhetorical structures and casual pronouns contain. If she truly performs the act of drawing conclusions, she risks opening up what is now conveniently shut. She therefore leaves us with an enigmatic closing, its tone provoking more than its brevity: "So this is my neighborhood. It's not the best but I can live with it." She does not press the issue of typicality, except that the phrase "this is my neighborhood" is the sort of plain, concluding gesture that a guide might use after a brief walking tour of any residential block. The last sentence seems to divide the world into "the best" and the tolerable and places her block in the latter category. Maria's tone betrays a touch of resignation to class difference, but it also shows her courage to normalize, to "live with it," that the drug paragraph dramatizes. She concludes by representing her reality as harsh but liveable, difficult but normal.

My English class discussed Maria's essay for a full fifty minutes, using our standard procedure of noting on the board all the topics and main points we found in the text—discovering what the essay was "about." I did not meet with her separately from the group, nor did I write any comments of my own on the paper although, as was my practice, I did participate in the class discussion, particularly in the last few minutes. Maria left the class surprised at all the issues we had found in her draft, determined to come back with a version that followed up on them:

10–25–88
[second draft]

My Neighborhood

For the past four and a half years, I've lived at 2003 north Hearst St. The block itself is alright. Sometimes it looks nice and at other times it can take on a totally opposite appearance. The homes have now taken on a new look. Well, most of them have but others haven't. Some have gotten new paint jobs and others have gotten new porches added to the front of their homes. But some people have done nothing to make their homes look better. They are mostly the people who live at the other end of my block. Also on my block, there is a very large garden. Helena Mendes is the name of the lady who owns it. She maintains it beautifully. During the summer she grows all kinds of vegetable. She also grows peach trees and many different types of roses and other kinds of flowers. Even though she had a very large fence she will arrange the wild violets vines that grows around the fence so it will make it virtually impossible to look into her garden. She loves her privacy whether it be in her home or even in her garden. But all in all the wild violets adds a beautiful touch to it. While she is carefully weaving the vines around the boards of the fence, she checks for any problems in the fence so she can fix them. Although I see her alot during the summer, she is the kind of person who keeps to herself.

A few of the people have put the extra light post in the front of their homes. At night I can just sit outside and just look at how the block is changing. But I regret that now that the weather is I won't be able to sit outside as long as I would like but I'll still be aware of the changes.

The people unlike the houses didn't change much in the past 4½ years. The friends I have live down my end of the street. A few of them I've known my whole life. The reason why I know is because my godparents owned a store on the corner on my block which is now an empty lot. That explains how I've know most of my friends for so long with only living here on this block for only four and a half years.

My friends are the kind of people you can talk to and feel comfortable. My cousin Lissette, who lives two houses away, and I used to have a serious talk about once a month just so we would be caught up with what was happening in each other's lives. We really had fun talking about school, parents and especially about the guys we met. But now that we are both Seniors we haven't seen much of each other. We both have got to work hard so that we can get good grades so that we can get into college.

But for the people who live farther up my block I really don't get along with. I've had situations when some of those girls would come up to me and try to act all sweet and innocent. But as soon as you turn your back they're always talking about you. Those very few people I really don't pay them any mind. Just as long as they stay out of my face. They are just a bunch of talk and no action.

As for the guys, I only truly hate one in particular. His name is Ramon. He's one who only talks when he's with his friends. In one situation about 2 years back he started to talk. He accused me and my friends of talking about him. As usual, he was with his buddies. I wasn't one who was going to let some stupid guy get over me. So if he would say something about me, his friends would laugh. So I would take whatever he said and send it right back at him and everyone would laugh. But then after he couldn't find anything else to do he left. His friends whom I know came to me and told me that he wasn't right and not to pay him any mind. I never did and ever since that day he's never said anything else to me.

Then there are those people who I do and don't know. I know them as where they live, their name and sometimes what car they drive. But I don't know what they do for a living and what they do when they go inside. If I see them on the street and I know that they are social, I'll say hi. But if they totally keep to themselves I usually let them be. But if they say hi I'll return it.

As for the drugs, you can find them around here But they are not on my immediate block. The major drug dealing corner is 5th and Norris. I myself know many of the people who work the corner. Fifth street used to be real quiet at night before the drugs started to infest it. I myself hate to see young guys sitting on some abandoned house's steps trying to sell someone a hit. They're not stupid. I've known a few of them from grade school and I know that they can do the work if they just set they're minds to it.

The thing that really trouble's me is that there is a young woman that sells drugs on fifth st. A few months ago she gave birth to a beautiful baby boy. I would think she would love that baby and give it all the motherly care that it so much needs. But two weeks about from Sun Oct 23 her baby died. I was waiting for the bus I saw her come out of her house crying. I didn't know what was happening. Then she started saying that her baby was dead. To me it seemed she was forcing herself to cry they say that her baby suffocated, the baby was about 2 months old. When the next time I saw her it was a few days after the baby's death, she seemed to be the happiest person on earth. I really don't think that she cared much for her baby. It seems that she is more con-cerned in selling drugs than taking care of her kids. A mother like that shouldn't be allowed to see her kids.

The addicts who come to buy drugs usually go to the first person they see. They just go up and ask them to sell them some-thing. This has happened to me a few times while I was waiting for the bus on that particular corner. I usually just look at them and send them up the block to the actually druggies. What else can I do?

To end my paper on the good side I'd like to talk about the trees on my block. I love this time of year because I love all the colors on the leaves. I love to watch the dry leaves being blown around and landing all over the place. I especially like to see the leaves after a shower. The leaves just stay there stuck as if put there forever. It's just so beautiful. But I only regret that autumn is so short and the leaves leave so quickly. If only it would last longer.

My dreams are like the leave. Here only a moment then blown away. But always the memory to stay in my heart.

This is, of course, the sort of revision that warms a writing teacher's heart. Besides being nearly four and a half times as long, it is far more exploratory and thoughtful than the first version while retaining the advantages of the first draft's neat organization. It has lost the earlier draft's focus on the typical or normal status of the neighborhood, but it makes up for losing that hazy thesis by frankly confronting issues that earlier she had stonewalled. Still, for my purposes I cannot afford merely to enthuse over Maria's revision. There are eloquences in the added detail, and new silences as well, which warrant a close account.

The second draft contains more mechanical slips and transcription errors, sentence fragments and awkward phrasings than her first version did. The questions it raises are sharper and more insistent, too. What does Helena Mendes's garden represent about the neighborhood? How does "the other end of the block" differ from her end? If there are no drugs on her block, how close is Fifth and Norris and how does this proximity affect the block? How do alliances and feuds affect the quality of life in the neighborhood, and what causes the tensions between and among people there? What "work" could the dealers do "if they just set they're minds to it"? Is the story about the young woman addict a cautionary tale or a representative anecdote? Does the ending suggest that her dreams are unattainable or idle? These are the questions one would ask the piece to answer if it were an article in a national magazine.

I read the errors, omissions, and new confusions as signs of a greater ambition. She is clearly less focused on surface manners and has invested more energy than she did before in representing a complex and elaborate reality, one open to the criticism and shocked disbelief of non-neighborhood readers. In short, Maria has taken the risk of showing her "difference," and in the process has taken on a greater role as representer and representative of her community.

This is not to say that the basic organization of the paper or the control over paragraph topic has diminished in effectiveness. If we make a list of the first sentences of each paragraph, including the topic sentence of the paragraph she mistakenly joined to her introduction, we have a reasonable outline of her paper:

1. For the past four and a half years, I've lived at 2003 north Hearst St.
2. Also on my block, there is a very large garden.
3. A few of the people have put the extra light post in the front of their homes.
4. The people unlike the houses didn't change much in the past 4½ years.
5. My friends are the kind of people you can talk to and feel comfortable.
6. But for the people who live farther up my block I really don't get along with.
7. As for the guys, I only truly hate one in particular.
8. Then there are those people who I do and don't know.
9. As for the drugs, you can find them around here But they are not on my immediate block.
10. The thing that really trouble's me is that there is a young woman that sells drugs on fifth st.
11. The addicts who come to buy drugs usually go to the first person they see.
12. To end my paper on the good side I'd like to talk about the trees on my block.
13. My dreams are like the leave.

Although the paper lacks an informing thesis, the paragraphs roll out in reasonable order, leading one to the other. The topic sentences are really quite commanding, with the paragraphs nicely fulfilling the promises made by the opening sentence in each. The fourth paragraph begins with a wonderful transition ("The people unlike the houses didn't change much"), one of those elegant guiding utterances one might expect from the voice-over in a TV documentary about Mozart's Vienna. It is, indeed, a bit too ingenious, betraying the fact that she has no underlying claim that would lend a compelling logic to the paragraphing order. Like many documentaries, it shrinks from taking a position on the material, but provides a marvelous look at the things and doings of its subject locale.

The progression from earlier to later draft in this project suggests a curious developmental pattern. At first, Maria's essay was dominated by a thesis made even more inflexible and restrictive by its less than explicit expression. Maria herself was probably not aware of the way the drive to portray her neighborhood as normal, typical, and unremarkable prevented her from developing any of the ideas and stories the essay touched upon. The thesis was preeminent though unexamined and thus not fully under the control of the writer. At the same time, Maria was so defensive about her neighborhood that she could not fully accept its authority to empower her to write extensively about its people and streets. This left her to offer only abstract principles, whose origins and implications were all but invisible to the reader.

In the second draft, Maria gives up defending her neighborhood so much and thus gains a greater authority to speak for the institutions that comprise it. She enters into its realities and brings it to life in written language, telling stories, describing scenes, and fleshing out the classification principles she had barely sketched originally. She gives up the tight control she had maintained at first in order to fulfill the role of representing the neighborhood to the reader. In so doing, her prose commits her to a greater identification with the neighborhood—she uses the first person more comfortably and expresses personal opinions and even personal quandaries ("What else can I do?")—and thus she presents herself as a representative member of the community she realizes through her writing. This is what sets her voice apart from the documentary narrator's voice. She may not have developed a thesis about the material, but she identifies more with the community than with an institution researching the community (television news, anthropology, sociology). Hers is now fully a voice from the chorus commenting upon the drama unfolding, rather than that of a dispassionate scientist investigating a site.

This shift raises an interesting pedagogical point. Writing teachers, and composition books, urge their students to develop a thesis. I see nothing wrong with the general practice, especially since Western readers have come to expect the explicit statement of the "point" to such an extent that writers must at least be aware of their readers' habitual way of reading. Moreover, one might assume that the ability to form a strong thesis would be a clear indication of the authority of a writer, her or his most direct expression of individual power. Yet the progress of Maria's paper is *away* from an explicit thesis, at least in this second draft. It may well be that in a third or fourth draft she could bring a specific position into focus, but I would argue that the crucial step is not the formation of a "main point" as much as the identification with an institution, or a complex of institutions, which can offer authority to the writer.

The journal entries and the interviews make clear Maria's active involvement with the realities of her family, friends, and neighborhood, but only when she can embrace those realities as sponsoring institutions can she write extensively. She must see that the institutions she knows best need representing more than they need her defensive silence, and she must come to see herself as an adequate representative of those institutions. The "point"—which is, among other things, a creature of school writing—can develop as she also comes to identify with the learned disciplines that demand it. For now she has transformed herself into an author by claiming authority from her home institutions. The sponsorship of my class served primarily to make a safe space within which those home institutions could take shape in her writing without being attacked as inappropriate, too "personal," or irrelevant to the "real" knowledge of textbooks and exams. At least in this instance, Neighborhood Academy's institutional authority formed a partnership with the home institutions Maria knew, and together we sponsored the writing project that Maria's neighborhood paper became.

Editing and Interviewing

Tita and Maria responded extremely enthusiastically to a number of assignments that were not traditional paper topics. Together they edited a tribute for a student who died suddenly early in 1989, and they also collaborated as coeditors for the school yearbook, finished in June of that year. In addition, they each took great pains over an assignment I gave my class to interview a person in their neighborhood. Both Maria and Tita came up with revealing and comprehensive interviews of boys they knew who had connections with the drug trade. I want to discuss their work on the editing and interviewing assignments briefly, for I think their responses add to the picture of authority I have been presenting.

On February 14, 1989—Valentine's Day—the school learned that a boy I will call here Stephen Jones had died suddenly over the weekend. We never learned the cause except that it was not related to drugs or street violence; it was just one of those seemingly divine decrees that sometimes take children away from us. The students and faculty were devastated. Stephen had been a very popular guy, with a penchant for playfulness that sometimes got him in trouble but endeared him to us nonetheless. Hoping to do something with all the emotions the students felt, I asked every English class to take time that day to write about their memories of Stephen and their grief at his loss. When the day was over, I had over sixty student responses to Stephen's death, but I didn't quite know what to do with them.

I talked to my class about the responses the next day, and we decided that we should put excerpts from the texts onto a single sheet for people to receive at the school memorial service the following day. Maria and Tita agreed to do the editing. Tita had had some experience with word processing and took to the computer work easily. I gave them the student writing and left them alone to mull over the texts, coming back throughout the day to help them think about their difficulties and answer any stray computer questions.

At the end of the day they had drawn up a moving document, a series of quotes that commemorated Stephen's energy and style and expressed the loss the students felt. Maria and Tita had been both judicious and generous, navigating the wide range of writing abilities and articulateness among the students while addressing the need for representing all elements in the school community. Here is the editors' note with which they concluded the tribute:

"When we were asked to edit this collection of thoughts and feelings about Stephen Jones, we accepted because Stephen was a very special person in our lives. We saw him every morning and had no choice but to love him. We hope that this collection helps you reflect back on all the memorable moments we had when Stephen was with us" ("In Loving Memory of Stephen Jones from his Family at Neighborhood Academy" [Feb. 16, 1989]).

The institutional role of an editor is more explicit than it is for a writer, and their note gives evidence that they recognize this role. Because they "were asked" to edit the collection by their teacher and by the administration of the school, they became agents of the school, capable of addressing the whole school community. However, they "accepted" this role, they say, out of personal and individual emotion. They thus occupy a position of mediating between private and public realities to produce written language that represents the private to the public, bringing tokens of the students' grief into the institutional record. They write that they hope the page "helps you reflect"; their goal was to produce a public representation of grief that could be used to substantiate the private emotional reality of the loss.

Maria and Tita did an equally responsive job on the school yearbook, a project that opened them up to a great deal more jealousy and second-guessing by their peers. I will omit a discussion of that large undertaking and merely note that both girls testified in an interview to the excitement and frustration of editing. What is perhaps more important than their remarks in the interview—they said they had learned about "organization" from their stint as editors—is the assurance in their voices and their commitment to the project once it went off to the printer. As Maria wrote in large letters in her journal the day we packed the manuscript up: "If this doesn't come out well you are going to see a very PISSED Puerto Rican. Watch Out!!"

At the risk of stretching a point, it seems significant to me that Maria would declare her investment in a school yearbook in terms of her identity as a Puerto Rican. I can't help but feel this is the strongest indication that the project mattered to her, and it suggests that the yearbook could only have worked for her if it had drawn not only on her identification with the school institution but also on her identity as a Puerto Rican. Not that projects needed to be directly tied to the Puerto Rican community—there is an unnecessarily limited scope to such "relevancy"—but projects can build on the collective sense of self-worth that a student derives from her community. A project framed so that it implicitly or explicitly excludes a student's origins from school institutional reality is a project doomed to fail for that student. A school whose institutional structure discourages the students from bringing their home allegiances into the learning process will likewise lose most of those students.

The interviews Maria and Tita produced were stunning. They chose fascinating people to interview, they asked challenging questions, and they followed up on issues their respondents glided over. Like editing, interviewing differs from the usual process of writing a paper, but both editing and interviewing highlight the element of decision making and control that an author needs to learn. An interview forces the writer to identify with a sponsoring institution; anyone who has ever watched TV news or sports knows that those interviews are always done under the auspices of a network, a specific program and, behind it all, a set of corporate sponsors. The interviewer draws her power to ask searching questions from the "public's right to know," as expressed through the entities of public media companies. An interview for school may feel at first a little artificial, but school works quite well as a substitute sponsoring institution for the corporations that sponsor network programming. Given a certain level of commitment on the part of the teacher, students easily respond to the challenge of interviewing.

I don't have the space here to discuss both girls' interviews, but Tita's interview serves well as an example of the work they did (in fact, most of the students in the class produced exceptional pieces for this assignment). She chose two brothers to interview. The elder brother— she calls him Mike—was a drug dealer at the time of the interview. The younger one was the "good" brother, supported by Mike and pressured by him to stay in school and out of the drug scene. Here is an excerpt from her interview with Mike:

> *What was your relationship with your brother like?*
> What can I say? He's my kid brother. You know, he's older now but I still like to think of him that way. We use to hang out all the time. He's alright. When I left home we still saw each other all the time. He's always been a good kid. That's never bothered me.
>
> *What do you think about your brother's choice to finish school?*
> It was his choice and I think it was the right one, you know. I didn't want him to get into drugs like me, so I'm glad that he didn't. I never thought that he would either.
>
> *Didn't you ever think that you would influence your brother to get into drugs?*
> Sometimes. But I told him that it was important for him to finish school. He looked up to me 'cause I was cool, you know.

Why was it important for him to make something of himself and not you?
'Cause he could do it and I never could.

Why couldn't you?
'Cause, you know, I didn't have the patience or time to learn and he always did.

Why did you get into drugs?
It was an easy way out of all of my problems. I always have money and I don't have to worry about taking care of my family 'cause I always make enough.

What's your family like?
Well, I got my old lady, my two boys, and one on the way.

How do you think your style of living will influence your children?
My kids won't get into drugs, 'cause I'm gonna push them to finish school. See, school wasn't for me, I just couldn't hack it. I know that my kids will make something of themselves. I'm not saying that school is a waste of time for everybody. It just was for me.

If you could go back in time and finish school, would you?
Nah, I don't think so.

Why wouldn't you?
'Cause I'm alright now, you know. I'm living well. And I got enough to take care of my kids with. Right now I'm problem free and that's the way that I want to stay.

Is there anything else that you would like to say?
Yeah . . . I wanted to tell you that I don't think of myself as a bad person. I mean I don't use drugs, I just sell them. I gotta make a living, you know? Selling drugs is the only thing that I know how to do, even though it's wrong.

Tita bravely pursues the subject of Mike's choices and his relationship to his brother and his own children. The first four questions in the above excerpt link one onto the next, pressing the issue of why one brother and not another could "make something of himself." This is a peculiarly linear line of questioning in a convoluted world—after all, it is the drug dealer who has "made something of himself," at least "enough to take care of my kids with" and to regard himself as "problem free." We could not expect for Tita to question all the contradictions of the situation, but she certainly raises some difficult questions for her interviewee to answer.

For both the concertedly casual interviewee and the restrained but persistent questioner, school stands as a symbol of the "good" path. Mike shrugs off his decision to drop out, but his answers reveal a conflicting picture of that decision. At one moment, he represents it as a reflection of his own failure ("I didn't have the patience or time to learn"), while at other moments he seems to see it as a wise and pragmatic career choice ("'Cause I'm alright now, you know"). In the end he feels compelled to address the contradiction squarely by asserting that he doesn't think of himself as a "bad person" despite his occupation and history. He makes no attempt to attack the school institution as corrupt or unresponsive to him. It was merely "a waste of time" for him.

Tita's attitude toward school authority is more unequivocally positive than Mike's, but it is tempered with an awareness of the realities outside the school walls. The questioner equates "making something of himself" with staying in school. She comes back to the question of dropping out with her hypothetical question "If you could go back in time. . . ," then follows up when his answer is too brief for her. She could just as easily have taken the line that school didn't seem to matter for Mike, and why was it necessary at all? Instead, she maintains an identification with the world of school, and asks her questions from that perspective. She clearly draws her authority as an interviewer from the school sponsor, yet she manages to ask her questions in a way that accepts the extra-curricular authority of her interlocutor. As one would expect from a girl who has grown up with drug dealers, she shows neither shock nor dismay at his story, while she maintains her position as a "good" student. Mike and Tita share a respect for the school's authority, but recognize its limits within the community.

The reader must not think that undertaking this interview was a simple matter for Tita. Here is a passage from her journal after she had done the interview:

Last night I went to church with my parents and halfway into the service a brother of the guys that I interviewed walked in. I was SURPRISED!!! (to say the least) I was hoping that he wouldn't say anything to me 'cause if my mom ever found out that I had interviewed a drug dealer, I would never hear the end of it. Well he said hi, how are you. My mom says you know this guy, and I said that we were introduced once. Whew!! I'm glad that she didn't find out. Boy am I lucky. (May 8, 1989)

The tension inside and outside Tita's house was so great, especially over the question of the "bad" influences outside her home, that Tita's attempt to interview someone from the "enemy" camp was courageous and independent. Until I read that journal entry, I had not been aware of just how difficult the interview assignment might be for my students.

Conclusion

Maria and Tita were successful students at Neighborhood Academy. They did their homework and showed up every day. They weren't disruptive or rude, and they could be depended upon to add to a discussion or hazard an answer to a teacher's most peculiar question. They were the sort of student that teachers want to requisition by the dozens from their principals at the beginning of every school year. Yet both Maria and Tita had failed out of high school elsewhere, and both used to shake their heads in conversations with me after school when I told them how well they were doing. "Oh, you should have seen us in our last school," they would say. Brats, they called themselves, *locas* or worse in the old days.

I cannot speak for Maria and Tita in their earlier years, nor do I presume to suggest an explanation for their learning styles across the curriculum. However, my study of their writing and interviews with me during the 1988–89 school year indicates that these were kids with great hope for what schooling could do for them but great fear that where they came from would prevent them from thriving anywhere outside their neighborhoods. The account of their year with me is the strongest argument I can make for the inseparableness of authority and social context.

I have said that their friendship was emblematic of the way they drew strength from a community network. I often thought about writing only on Maria or only on Tita, but I could never get very far without

bringing in something that the excluded friend had said. This is a tribute to their friendship, but it is also an indication of the extent to which
their writing can be best appreciated if we understand something about
the social dynamics within which they wrote. In short, the two girls
needed each other. Maria and Tita each faced quite distinct challenges
in their home and neighborhood lives. Yet, as school writers, they each
faced the prospect of leaving behind most of what they "knew" in order
to venture further in the academic world.

Maria and Tita's writings in my class which showed the greatest
richness and detail was associated with their lives outside school. This
is not to say that Maria and Tita did not write essays on more standard
school topics, but none of them approached the exploratory vigor of
the journal writing or the work on their neighborhoods. This undoubtedly reflects my own bias as a teacher and a researcher—I was looking
for ways to contextualize their writing, for them and for me—but I
think it also reflects the resources they had for representing reality in
written language. For the sake of comparison, let me present an in-class
essay Maria wrote for me on her final exam:

> *Who was Frederick Douglass and why should American students
> know his work?*
>
> Frederick Douglass was a black man enslaved for the thought
> that this was right (in the mind of a white man)
>
> Frederick Douglass is also a very brave man. He is brave in
> the sense that he didn't let anything get in his way to stop him
> from reading and writing. He did this even though he knew what
> would happen to him if he was caught.
>
> Secondly he was brave to write his life story. He literally gave
> himself up. He knew what he was doing and he still did it. I admire
> him for doing that. Not many people would do that today. He
> should be remembered for that one deed.
>
> Students should read his work because his is an inspiration to
> all. He shows how badly someone needs an education. People
> today give up the oppurtunity of learning to read and write. FD
> wasn't pushed to go to school, he pushed himself. He didn't let
> anything or anyone stop him. He should be a major example to
> all (June 12, 1989)

The essay question is, of course, calculated to elicit not only specifics about the book but connections between the book and the life students live. Maria responds by giving me what I ask for. She starts out with a very clever idea about contrasting images in the mind of white and black men, but she can't quite succeed in unpacking the concept. She then focuses on ways that Douglass can serve as "an inspiration" for American students. In this effort she does succeed, at least in so far as she communicates her own enthusiasm for Douglass as a model.

The problem with my question, and Maria's response, is that in many ways it does not ask her for what she knows best. I suppose that to draw mainly upon her institutional authority, I should have asked her to discuss three instances in the book that she thought would appeal to friends on her block. How, for instance, would she explain her excitement about Frederick Douglass to Lissette, her cousin? Or, perhaps more challenging yet, what passage would she choose for Felix's mother to read if she wanted to show Delores what was so special about Douglass's book? Is there something that Douglass says that could keep Maria's brother from dropping out of school? Putting the final exam aside, I would personally love to hear Maria's answer to those questions.

Nevertheless, I would not write a more personalized exam question for Maria or any other student at Neighborhood Academy. Everything I have said in this chapter about Maria and Tita's authority as writers I believe to be valid and essential for teachers and composition theorists to take into account, but in a real sense it is only the first half of the story. The other half of the story is that many of Maria and Tita's fears about college are well founded, though the obstacles are not nearly as insurmountable as they seem to a high school student from North Philadelphia. College essay questions on Frederick Douglass, or even on the sociology of the Puerto Rican community of Philadelphia, will not as a rule ask Maria and Tita to identify themselves with their home communities as they write. The professors will ask students to identify themselves with the discipline of the course—literary criticism, sociology, political science—and the authority to make distinctions and order arguments must be drawn more or less exclusively from what they have learned about academic institutional life. I do not attack the professors for the rhetorical frame of their questions; it is a reasonable artifact of the institutional structure within which the professors themselves operate. In my final chapter, I will consider the implications for pedagogy and composition theory of the institutional terrain that authors like Maria, Tita, and Kareem must traverse.[3]

Maria and Tita must find a way to translate the power they feel within their home lives into a new sort of power within an entirely different social matrix. Perhaps this translation may be easier for Tita than for Maria. Tita drew comparatively more support from her school than from her home life. Once she found a school that validated her as a contributing member, she seemed to embrace that new world, especially since Neighborhood Academy did not ask her to renounce her allegiance to her Puerto Rican origins. She did, in fact, graduate in 1990 at the head of her class, and was accepted at a Catholic college in the Philadelphia area.

Maria, on the other hand, had more positive reasons to maintain her place within the families she came from. Maria did not leave home for college after graduation, much to the chagrin of her teachers. She stayed at home the following year, having taken a deferred admission at the college that accepted her. In February of the following year, she and Felix broke up. A week after their break-up, Maria called me to ask for help getting her place back in the college; she was afraid they would not want her anymore since she hadn't called the admissions office all year. Her mother was at first quite hostile to Maria starting college, saying that Maria would never succeed, that she could never "make anything of herself." But the day Maria left for her reentry interview, her mother drove her to the trolley stop and waited with her for the trolley. Maria told me that it turned out her mother's greatest worry was that Maria would be attacked on the public transportation. "Why do you want to go so far away from home?" her mother asked her. The school Maria chose is not outside the Philadelphia city limits.

---

3. Without jumping ahead to the ideas contained in the final chapter, I would like to say that I do not regard the method or plan of the English course I taught that year to be exemplary or even remarkable. This book makes no claim to show other teachers the way to structure better college preparatory courses for urban high school students. Looking back on what I did in that course, I think I would change much of the reading and assignments I used that year except for journal writing and the neighborhood paper. Now I know a bit more about what I am looking for as I try to help writers develop a sense of authority, and I have used my experiences at Neighborhood Academy a great deal since then, but I do not claim to have known what I was doing in any special way the year I taught Maria, Tita, and Kareem. As a friend used to say to me, the time to write a seminar paper is after you've taken the seminar. I hope I'm a better teacher now for having done this study.

4

. . . .

Kareem

Kareem was a seventeen-year-old African-American senior from a calm residential neighborhood called East Mount Airy. He lived with his mother and two older brothers. Although his family was in better financial circumstances than many students who went to Neighborhood Academy, his profile as a student was quite typical. He came to Neighborhood Academy in his junior year after he had begun to do poorly in his local public high school, skipping school and failing classes. At Neighborhood Academy, he attended school regularly and brought his grades up to a modest C average. The teachers recommended him for my class not because his writing was so special—even among the boys in the school he was not the most skilled writer—but because he had a positive attitude toward school and enjoyed class discussions. I believe he was pleased and proud, in general, to be in an accelerated college preparatory class in 1988–89 because he hoped to go on to college and a military career.

Kareem is a difficult writer to write about. Although he and I grew close during the school year, he was never anywhere near as open with me as Maria and Tita were. Other students in my class that year were more forthcoming in interviews and journal writing, and perhaps others would have suited my theories of authority better. But the more I looked at the class material after the year was over, the more I felt the need to come to terms with Kareem's writing. He was reticent, elusive, and downright frustrating much of the time. City teachers run into young men in their classes often who won't talk, won't open up. I make no claim that Kareem is typical, but I think it may help teachers to hear a reading of writing by a student who, despite his "good" behavior in class, basically resisted school.

101

I think my story of Kareem is a story of an authority-less author. Although Kareem wanted desperately to appear "strong" in his writing, he had very little social ground upon which to develop authorized texts. In the first section of this chapter, I will review Kareem's journals and the personal context of his work in 1988–89. I will suggest that Kareem displays in his writing a remarkable passivity toward events and identifies with social institutions largely as a consumer. In the second section, I will look at three drafts of a paper describing his neighborhood. I had designed the neighborhood assignment so that the school would share the role of authorizing institution with the students' home communities, hoping that Neighborhood Academy students would then feel freer to become authors as well as a writer. What I find in this section is that in the first two drafts Kareem's writing remains sketchy, in large part because he doesn't identify himself with any institution closely enough to represent its picture of reality or to present himself as an institution's representative.

In the third and final draft of his neighborhood paper, Kareem does take on the role of representative of his neighborhood. Surprisingly for me, the extensiveness of his prose and the relative sophistication of his authority also disconcerts me, for I recognize I forced him to undertake challenges to his sense of belonging in the process of becoming an author. This chapter is perhaps more a portrait of me as a writing teacher than it is a characterization of Kareem as a student writer.

Some readers may feel in the course of my discussion about Kareem that I am appropriating his words to tell a story that may not be Kareem's. Maria and Tita spoke a great deal to me, and if I had questions about why they wrote certain ways, or why they took certain social positions in class, I could ask them. The chapter I wrote about them was thus heavily informed by their own words, by their attitudes, even by their laughter and tears. But Kareem was a much more private person, and thus my story about him must be more speculative and even, perhaps, imagined. He would sometimes stay after school to talk, and occasionally I would meet him on the street near my home, since he lived only a few blocks from my house in West Mount Airy. Our conversations, however, were much more a matter of external doings—jobs to do, future plans, gossip about kids we both knew. Occasionally Kareem would tell me about a girlfriend he'd broken up with, or worries he had about his health.

I admit to my readers right now that this chapter is about the *image* of Kareem I came to adopt in order to read his papers. I can say that in general my way of reading Kareem's writing seemed to fit the words he wrote, and he never told me I was off base in my comments on his writing. I do believe he wrote more fluently and confidently after my course, and his greater fluency may be evidence that my approach to him was based on a relatively accurate picture of who he was as a student. What I offer here makes some sense out of our interactions and his written words and may serve as a basis for further work with students who, like Kareem, write a prose that seems to omit more than it says. But I would be dishonest to say that this chapter represents Kareem's thinking about his writing. Instead, I present in the following pages my best reading of Kareem's writing in the year that I taught him. This is at least as much my story as it is his.[1]

Journal and Context

Kareem's writing life in my class began with his answers to a questionnaire:

> *Describe something about yourself you think is distinctive or special.*
> One caracteristic that is special about me is my ability of strong thinking and strong criticism.
> *Describe your attitude toward writing.*
> Well if I have to write I do it, one the other hand I like to write about strong subjects that have many points of views, so that I can issue mine.
> *Describe your best writing experience.*
> My best writing experiences is when I discribe someone or something.

---

1. Once again, I fear that the warnings and hedges I have put in the opening paragraphs of this chapter will not satisfy those who worry about my coopting the voices of students. As I note here, Kareem is a particularly challenging student to bring into this study, but I cannot let the narrative problems prevent me from telling the story. I have assembled here a version of his texts and a characterization of this young man, whom I call Kareem. Perhaps I am acting more like a novelist than a researcher in telling his story. If we teach literature in schools as a form worthy of contemplation, I don't see why we can't spare a place for studies that present closely reasoned "fiction" as one teacher's approximation of truth.

Describe your worst writing experience.
My worst writing experience is when the teacher issues a boring subject.

What would you like to get out of English this year?
I would like to be a better reader and writer because I and very creative and I can learn to understand many things.

Write a short essay about your hopes and dreams for the future.
About 10 years from know I think I would like to own my own business. Maybe own a limozine service or to be a contractor of some type. Although my main goal in life if I go to college is to become a military loyar. If I Don't go to college, I want to be a military officer who recrouts people.

What I find interesting about this first piece is how much power is evident as a theme. The characteristic he stresses in the first answer is strength. He doesn't make clear whether "strong" means dearly held opinions or vehement arguing powers, but here—as elsewhere in school life—Kareem's concept of himself as "strong" is central. "Strong" is repeated in the second answer to describe the kind of writing he likes to do. Notice that the "one the other hand" distinguishes "strong subjects" from times where "if I have to write I do it." I suppose the distinction he has in mind is between assignments teachers force on him (the "boring subjects" that "the teacher issues" in his worst writing experiences) and ones which, though assigned, appeal to him or allow him to express an opinion he already has.

The picture which emerges from this brief piece of writing is already one of a battlefield where teachers "issue" subjects and Kareem "issues" his "strong" responses. The use of the word "issue" is not merely a result of an underdeveloped vocabulary. He surely knows more common words that might work there, such as "give" or "assign" or even "contribute." "Issue" is a military word—Kareem was very interested in the military—and the connotations of equipment and commands assigned to personnel are quite apt for the reality Kareem is representing here.

I must concede that Kareem was a terrible speller. He never improved much, no matter what I said, although he did admit to me that he was self-conscious about his spelling. He also persisted in making those little mistakes that annoy teachers so much—"one" for "on," "and" for "am," and an anomalous capital "D" in the middle of the last sentence of the hopes and dreams paragraph. All this coming from a guy who could produce a perfectly well-punctuated, complex sentence like "If I Don't go to college, I want to be a military officer who recrouts people." After spending a year with Kareem in my class, I can only conclude that he stubbornly refused to clean up such errors because it represented a type of power he had in the situation. The big "D" in "if I Don't go to college" may express anxiety—although he always capitalized R, usually M and N, and occasionally B, D, and S—but I would prefer to avoid the psychoanalysis of his errors. Except in a few papers that he did become invested in despite himself, it was enough for him that he did "my" work—to take pride in it too would have been to overspend personal energy in a project that didn't belong to him.

In his answer to the best experience question, he doesn't mention a teacher or assignment—to describe "someone or something" can be a task the writer controls himself. But I didn't realize until I sat down with all of Kareem's writing after the year was over just how accurate and revealing that one little sentence was. Description, indeed, was his preferred mode. His journal was almost entirely composed of description and a bare chronicle of the events in his life and his neighborhood. There is very little attempt to question why something happened or to consider someone's motivation for an action. In fact, his journal presents a world which, like the world of writing assignments, is issued by someone else.

We started every class with five to seven minutes of journal writing, usually with no specific topic assigned. Since Kareem was late for school a great deal during the 1988–89 school year, and my class was the first of the day for him Monday through Thursday, he missed journal writing more often than others—his journal has 51 pages filled, while the student with the best attendance filled 107 pages. But when he was there for journal writing he got quite involved with it, and sometimes, if I let him, he would continue writing for the first few minutes of my introductory remarks. A cast of characters unfolded in his journal as in few others'; he seemed intent on recording the goings and doings of his "boughs" (his spelling of "boys," the "homeboys" he hung out with) from the neighborhood, some of whom traveled with him to school. One of the preoccupations of his journal was what clothing and jewelry he and his friends bought, and how much they paid for it all. Another theme in the journal was who was irritated with whom over what occurrence; the issues were hardly ever noted.

A major element of Kareem's reality that the journal represents is the extent to which things *happened* to him rather than Kareem being the agent of action. The first entry of the journal provides a good example:

> When I woke up this morning I just knew that I would Be on time for school. I hopped in the Shower with the quickness, stay there for about five minuates.
> After I got out of the shower I started to get dressed. By the time I was ready to leave it was 7:20 A.M. and I was suppose to get a ride with Rone and his pop. When I got to Rone's house the van was gone so I thought they left me. So I went on the ave to my cousens house to get him. He was still there. My cousin and I went to WAWA to get breakfast before we went to school. When we came out of Wawa, Rone and Charlie were walking up the Street

Rone, Charlie, and Kareem's cousin all went to school at Neighborhood Academy, which is a good forty-five minutes to an hour away from Kareem's neighborhood by public transportation, though by car you can make it in twenty to thirty minutes if you are lucky and no trolley is broken down along your route. Kareem approaches the problem of getting to school on time as a matter of fate—this day he just happened to wake up with the feeling that he'd make it, and my attendance record shows that he did. Rone's father was going to drive them to school; thus 7:20 A.M. was not a bad time to get out of the house to make the 8:30 A.M. bell. The van had seemingly disappeared—no anger or surprise or panic—and this would seem to call for an alternate plan of travel, commencing immediately. Kareem not only did not rush to a bus or trolley, but he went to his cousin's house, and then stopped at the store for breakfast. When Rone and Charlie showed up, his neck was saved. Presumably the van hadn't left and all was well.

The innocent teacher reading this entry might think: Oh well, Kareem has a lackadaisical attitude toward lateness, and he probably doesn't have the skills to express the emotional drama of thinking he'd been left behind. I should note that Neighborhood Academy specializes in getting chronic truants to come to school on time, and for every one of Kareem's latenesses he had to pay back time in detention after school, which he did not like. In addition, even early in the year, the principal and vice-principal were already on his back to improve his attendance record in order to ensure his graduation. Kareem was not an expressive writer, but a careful reader can note in his writing samples above a number of dependent clauses subordinated by "after," "when," "although," and "if," which display his skills with transitions and dramatic effect. He was capable of making hierarchical arrangements of information, but, when he related a story, events more often than not were yoked by a simple "and." His verbal excuses followed this same pattern: arrangements and promises others had made just never worked out quite right and, according to him, his best intentions to change often didn't materialize through no fault of his own. This pattern of being acted upon asserts itself as a steady element in Kareem's world view throughout the journal.

Incidents of this theory of causation abound in Kareem's writing. When he is late he doesn't blame anyone, but it never occurs to him, as he records his stops at the store or at what point in his bus connections he got stuck, that specific actions made him late. The best he can do is repeat high-level promises like the one he made in February: "Yesterday I came to school late and to my surprise Mr. T—— and Mr. M—— would not let me in. Not being able to get in school really hurt me. For some reason I think that it's gona hurt alot more in the future. I told them it will never happen agin" (Feb. 28, 1989). It is curious that he uses the word "hurt," rather than "mad" or "frustrated." And the principal and vice principal surprise him with their action, which seems to Kareem rather unilateral. They did something *to* Kareem in this formulation, and although he says "it" will never happen again, his language suggests that he still doesn't see that lateness was not something external that happened to him.

School performance also elicited this sort of response. In anticipation of my first confrontation with him over his academic performance, Kareem wrote:

Today Mr. Gollblat is very angry with me. He said that he wants to talk to me after school. I have a good idea why. But I'm not gona say. I'll just see what he has to say.

I know that I'm behind and I plan to amerge, but its just that
I have things on my mind that some people just don't understand,
Even if I tried to explain them.
What I plan to do is just do what I have to do to make it
through. Just take my word, when June comes I will be fling by
with Flashing Colors. (Oct. 27, 1988)

His relationship with me as a reader is very interesting in the journal, for he names the teacher and refers to me as "he," yet he doesn't
want to say what his idea of the issue is in the journal. Perhaps he
doesn't want to prejudice his case with me, or perhaps he just doesn't
want to make his school problems too real by writing them down. He
seems always to note the positive and suppress the negative, using the
journal as a place only to represent himself as one who will change and
"amerge." Here, as in other places, Kareem often chose silence as a
response to a challenge or an objection to his behavior. I think he
honestly felt that silence, rather than excuse or explanation or calls for
help, was the strong and honorable response to trouble.

He alludes to the idea that "some people" would not understand
what was on his mind, but the teachers at Neighborhood Academy had
the reputation for understanding student problems—that's why Kareem and his friends were coming from across the city to attend the
school. Not being understood was not the issue, but not being able to
name the problem was. Kareem had tremendous difficulty saying what
was bothering him, although his journal proves that he could write
fluently and with a vocabulary certainly adequate to describe situations
around him. Perhaps he didn't trust me or anyone else at the school,
but my sense was there was something much larger than individual trust
at stake. I don't believe he wanted what was bothering him to enter
the official reality that writing or speaking about his problems would
bring about.

As for the "things" on his mind, they may well have existed without
being named either in journal entries or conversations. However, I
know from experience with students who have serious problems weigh-
ing on them that when they are prepared to take responsibility for their
lives, the problems get named, and once they are named they are usually
not the impediment they seem. Kareem was not prepared to take the
step of naming his problems and taking responsibility for his school

performance beyond intermittent claims like "I've got a new Attitude" (Nov. 1, 1988) or "One thing I know is that it all up to me. So I feel that it is time to make my move" (Dec. 8, 1988). In the middle of a period when the journal was full of accounts of girl problems—surely one of the big "things" on his mind, as he once admitted to me—he wrote: "My birthday is the 8th of next month. I will be 18 years old and I plan to come out a little bit better by doing what I have to do, because I have really been falling behind in school and I am so ashamed of myself" (Mar. 29, 1989).

There is no more concrete plan in the March 29, 1989, passage than there was in the October 27, 1988, passage where he said that he would "do what I have to do to make it through." "Doing what you have to do," which is an expression a football coach might use, is in keeping with the military metaphor that the teacher "issues" a challenge and the student responds. This is the reality that most students live with in their school life, but for Kareem it was a dysfunctional metaphor, especially in conjunction with his perception of himself as a victim of events. It made him passive, unable to see any writing project as personally valuable, and it made him feel ashamed of himself without giving him a reasonable prospect of changing his luck. Even as late as June, Kareem was still approaching the system according to hunches and intuitions. When I asked him, two weeks before school was letting out, if he would come to see me after school, he wrote: "I guess he's gona tell me that I'm gona fail his class. I really can feel it coming." In fact, I gave him a list of assignments to do so that he wouldn't fail my class and would be able to graduate. He did enough to squeak by, but he never gave a convincing show of understanding just how much he controlled his own failure and success.

When Kareem had successes in school, they too seemed to come from nowhere. In his first marking period, his grades were better than he expected. Here was his response:

> Guess what I just found out. Through guessing, I made 2nd Honors for the Hole school this report period. Rone also made it, but Charlie and Stan didn't. I don't know why Charlie didn't make them because he is very smart and he says that he does all of his work. Although I can believe why Stan didn't make it, because I heard that he plays in class, doesn't do his work and I know that he has missed alot of days in school.

As for me I can't wait to get home to tell my mom and get some money from her. I plan to buy my temberlands.

He had apparently had a conversation with his homeroom teacher in which he guessed that he had made second honors, but it sounds here like the guessing *got* him second honors. He does understand why another student might not get good grades, but the system still seems like a minor mystery to him—yet one that is not worth much more than a thought, before turning to the money rewards his grades will bring. But these rewards are more like the jackpot in a slot machine because, despite the apparent arrangement with his mom that good grades bring money, Kareem seldom expressed any anxiety or jubilation about a grade on an assignment—whether it was an F or a B.

Perhaps the most striking example of Kareem's luck approach to events was what happened the day we had arranged for him and another student to go for an interview at a state school outside Philadelphia called Kutztown University. He had a good chance of getting into the school, or so I gathered from the admissions officer, and Kareem seemed excited about Kutztown. The other student's mother had agreed to drive them both up there. All Kareem had to do was meet James and his mother at the corner of Broad and Olney at a certain time in the morning. Here's how he described that morning:

> Yesterday was a very humiliating day for me. It started off on a bad foot and I knew it would end on a bad foot. I was *supposed* to meet James up Broad and Olony at 7:00 A.M. I arrived there at 6:50 A.M. As time went by I knew He should of been there. The moral of the story is He never came. (May 4, 1989)

He says the experience was "humiliating," although he doesn't say why. The way he puts the "moral" of the story, one would think Kareem should be mad. What he doesn't say is that James *had* been there at the right time—across the street from where Kareem was standing. Kareem had stood and waited, but had not bothered to consider what might have gone wrong and how he could try other alternatives to find his ride. Indeed the moral *was* that "He never came"—that is the sort of lesson from occurrences which Kareem tended to draw.

Kareem did finally get to Kutztown by bus, but the result wasn't good. He was rejected soon after the interview. I called up the admissions officer to ask what had gone wrong. He said Kareem had done very poorly on the placement tests in math and English, although Kareem himself had said they were amazingly easy. But the admissions officer, who is black and quite experienced with inner-city students, said that the interview with Kareem had been the least favorable element of his visit. Kareem just hadn't seemed to the interviewer like someone who wanted to go to college. He wasn't forthcoming with answers to questions, he didn't show much interest in the programs or course offerings, and he seemed to the interviewer to be hostile and defensive. They had decided that with all the students who were applying for special admissions under state-mandated remedial categories, they didn't need a guy who didn't seem to care.

I did not puzzle over Kareem's performance on the placement tests. I had coached him on the sort of math he was likely to see, and I saw that he knew basic computations and could also do algebraic manipulations at least well enough to qualify him for a pre-college booster program, but he could not be consistent at solving problems without making petty errors or forgetting a crucial step. I had spent a good deal of class time in English working on how to produce a standard college application essay and had tutored him, in addition, on the particulars of Kutztown's exam. Yet I knew when he sat down to write he would not think out an argument, would not consider the question, and would probably not even reread his answer to check for spelling and punctuation errors. Like so much else this year, for Kareem the college application process was simply off on a "bad foot."

Kareem used this same eerie sense of things happening as a mere chain of events to describe situations which did not directly involve him:

Today I have a super head ace. It all started last night over sams house. But any way what I want to talk about is last Friday My friend Frank and My Brother Sid were in McDonalds and Frank got into a fight with Jeff from Stenton Ave. He hit Jeff twice and through him out of the McDonalds Window. The next day roomer was that Sid & Frank roled on Jeff.

One o'clock Sunday morning Frank is up stairs in his apartment with Teanka, I thought Fred was up there too. Jeff and

someone else through a fire ball in Frank's house, it cought fire.
Frank and Teanka got out the side window. As for the House,
"It's totaled (Nov. 14, 1988)

The story needs a bit of background information. Sid is a few years
older than Kareem and had also been at Neighborhood Academy, although he had been kicked out for being an uncooperative and violent
presence at the school. I had not known Sid, but the present vice-
principal assured me it would surprise him if Sid had witnessed a fight
and been content simply to watch. Thus, the last sentence of the first
paragraph is more significant than it looks because it is a modest defense
of Kareem's brother's honor. To roll on somebody is to gang up on
him; hence, the rumor Kareem reports is a bad reflection on Sid and
Frank's reputation: to fight two against one would be cowardly. But
fights of this kind don't materialize out of nothing, especially if they
are followed by firebombs. There is much to this story that is suppressed
and muted, and the action appears unmotivated, inexplicable.

There does seem to be a cause and effect proposed here—if you
throw somebody through a window, be prepared for violent consequences—but there is a strange, smokeless clarity to the action. No fuss
or anger, no fear, and emphatically no mention of complicating factors
such as gang territory or jealous rivalries or drug dealing. One goes to
Sam's house and develops a headache; one goes to Frank's house and
gets firebombed. Of course, Kareem is writing this in school and under
time constraints, but I doubt whether he is keeping information from
me. In an earlier entry he revealed the secret of a card trick he was
planning to run on fellow students to make some extra money, so I
suspect he was not always conscious that what he said in the journal
might be spilling the beans. I think he saw it as a natural outcome of a
fight that one party would punch another, and what follows a punch is
then more or less inevitable. Frank himself seems, in the above account,
hardly responsible for the events of the story; one might just as well
blame McDonald's for allowing customers to congregate while waiting
for their orders.

Franchises like McDonald's and street names like Stenton Avenue
and malls like "C-the-Brook Mall" (formally called Cedarbrook) and
brand names like Timberland are, along with the ever-present SEPTA
(Southeastern Pennsylvania Transit Authority), the social institutions

that weave their way through the personal drama represented in Kareem's journal. Like the characters in *The Sun Also Rises,* who are forever ordering and eating sumptuous meals while drinking vast quantities of conspicuously labeled alcohol, Kareem and his friends are described in his journal as forever buying gold rings and gold ropes and watches and boots and pants and coats. Unlike the wealthy set in Hemingway's book, these kids must spend all the money they make in their after-school jobs in order to keep up the consumption, borrowing money from each other when they can, putting things on layaway when they can't. One sequence of entries tells the story of the ups and downs of Kareem getting a removable gold cap to slip onto his tooth, and another tells the story of a pair of eyeglass frames that came to him in a trade but were smashed somehow.

This endless round of consumption is yet another representation of a paradoxical kind of victimization. I have a photograph of Kareem with a few other students. He is sitting in the front row, looking terribly proud of himself, sporting five rings and a pair of designer eyeglass frames. One can just make out the huge ring with a money sign that he always wore. At one point in the year, the vice-principal, who was black, suggested to Kareem he ought not to wear so much gold to school. Kareem was outraged by the administration's policy against his style—"Are they against my looking Black?" he wrote in his journal. No one could tell him that his blackness did not depend upon a look styled after drug dealers, who wear gold in case they need sudden access to cash. Clearly the pursuit of *things* that permeates his journal was an important part of his public persona, of his claim of being a person of respectable standing in the community. In the process, he and his friends not only spent every cent they had and much that their parents would give them, but they also bought cheap and shoddy products sold by street merchants and store owners quite happy to oblige their habit.

I am nearly certain that neither Kareem nor any of his closest friends at Neighborhood Academy were into the drug trade. Kareem worked hard after school to afford material possessions that would bring him status among his peers. He didn't expect to earn status in any other way. The gold he bought represented his constant claim of strength and ambition, but his preoccupation with buying revealed his lack of confidence that he could ever be anything to society except a consumer.

Perhaps the most characteristic relationship Kareem had with an

institution was with SEPTA. At the end of October, Kareem had a bad
accident on public transportation. Here's how he described the event:

> Just last Friday I had an actcident of a Septa bus. I was on the H
> Bus going to lincoln Drive and Mount Pleasant Ave. I pulled the
> lever to signal my stop. My friend Scott and I both got up. He
> was standing at the Back do waiting to get off and I was walking
> tward the front Door. As I was still in motion to the front door,
> the bus Driver sort of jammed on the brakes. The next thing I
> knew, I woke up calling my friend scott. He said "I'm here, can
> you get up."

Now, bus accidents are one of those things that people in the city
talk about like lottery jackpots. Some people literally spend years going
to doctors and lawyers, hoping that something that happened to them
on public transportation will support them for the rest of their lives.
Kareem's accident was, I think, quite real, and though he did go to a
lawyer and had his case going for much of the year, I don't think he
or his family expected to get rich from a suit or settlement. I have seen
students at Neighborhood Academy whose families were trying to cash
in on SEPTA accidents; it is nearly a full-time job which requires many
days of absences for the sake of court appearances and doctor's ap-
pointments. This accident seriously shook up Kareem—he later told
me he could never stand up on a bus without bracing himself carefully,
and even then he was always afraid of falling—but he never mentioned
the bus accident again in the journal, except in the next day's entry
about a visit to the physical therapist. He wore a neck brace off and on
for the next few months, but I believe he dropped his lawsuit when we
pointed out to him that he could not on the one hand claim a disability
and on the other hand expect to enlist in the marines.

The bus accident was just the kind of occurrence Kareem didn't
need, for it reinforced his sense that things happened to him that he
could neither control nor prevent. It exacerbated the split view he had
of himself. On the one hand he saw himself as a strong guy, both
physically and mentally. He was a fullback for his local community football team—he described his career to me in glowing detail in a midterm
exam question which was supposed to be a mock-up of a college application essay—and he was built powerfully, although he was not big.
He was devoted to a picture of himself as a future marine officer, and

he carried his head high when he walked. He also thought of himself as smart and able to speak his mind and was often aggressive in class discussions, especially in the beginning of the year.

Yet Kareem must have had serious doubts about himself in exactly those areas he proclaimed as his strengths. He never did anything more physical than walk up the stairs in school—didn't go out for the basketball team, or play wallball during lunch break, or help set up chairs for assemblies, or volunteer to carry things. In a tiny school like Neighborhood Academy, it wasn't hard to recognize someone who liked to show off his strength and physical prowess, and we had plenty of guys who were in that category. As far as a career in the marines, Kareem seemed relatively unsuited for a service that prides itself on toughness and discipline. Unlike the students we had who did go into one or another service, he was squeamish about blood or injuries either to others or himself, hated to take orders, and was extremely sensitive to what male authority figures thought of him.

In class, his comments often seemed to be willful attempts to block intellectual engagement. I remember a discussion we had in a science class I taught one day when the teacher was absent. Kareem insisted that we couldn't really "know" that the earth doesn't grow like a living thing—after all, volcanoes were like blood spurting out and rocks were like bones. Not that he was mocking or being intentionally silly; he just didn't want to accept the distinction between metaphorical and scientific thinking. He was truly angry at me that day when I finally changed the subject because from his point of view I hadn't answered his objections to the discussion. From my point of view there had been no discussion; we had been talking about two different worlds and Kareem's world played by a set of rules the rest of us could only guess at.

His third entry of the year, and in some ways his saddest, reads as follows:

Yesterday, I had a boy. When I first heard it, it was from my mom. It didn't seem like much when I heard it so all I did was want to sleep. When I woke up I called the mothers house she was in the hospital sence late last night. Her brother came to my house to take me to the Hospital.

When we got to the hospital it was about 9:05 P.M. and visiting hours were over, but since I'm the father I could go to her room.

Kareem's reaction that "all I did was want to sleep" was characteristic. Whether he meant he "went" to sleep or not doesn't much
matter—the fact is he probably very much *wanted* to sleep after the
news. I know from a long conversation we had soon after this entry
that the news affected him more than he let on in the journal entry,
but basically he experienced the child's birth as something that the girl
had done to him, to try to hold him. He felt that if he was ever going
to help his son, he would have to do it by making something of himself,
but he didn't know how he was going to do that, so the whole prospect
just frightened him into inaction. To be sure, he was a little proud—as
we see in the last line of the entry. Being a father, he could break the
normal rules, which he challenges by coming to the hospital so late in
the first place (he seems to have depended on the mother's brother to
get there at all).

This is the last entry in the journal that mentions the child or, as
far as I know, the mother, except that on January 5, 1989, he mentions
a trip downtown: "I plan to buy my son something & also I plan to
buy myself something. I want a pair of black jeans and a pair of red or
white jeans." The specificity of the plan for his own shopping suggests
that the gift for his son is more an obligation than a compelling reason
for the trip. Given the date, the gift for his son is probably a Christmas
present he had not managed to buy earlier—elsewhere in the journal
·he mentions times when he was in trouble for not having presents to
give people on their birthdays.

My relationship with Kareem is particularly pertinent to this study.
He grew more and more suspicious of my work as the year went on—
he always told me he had a "phobia" about being taped, and in fact
he only let me tape an interview once. At one point, I made the mistake
of talking him into an interview with an artist who came to the school
to shoot a documentary about Neighborhood Academy. He agreed to
the interview, but later felt so invaded by it that I asked the artist to
erase her tape on him, which she did. For a month or so after that, I
blamed myself for his reticence in class, but after a while I realized that
the taped interview had been less crucial in itself than it was sympto-
matic of a large-scale problem. It had represented for a him the very
real threat that writing exposed him to: recording his thoughts and
feelings in a way that other people might see them and hold him to
them.

Late in the year, he wrote in response to a set of summation questions that "You may have the rest of the students blind, but not me." I asked him when I read his paper if he was mad at me for my study. What did he think I was trying to do to the students? At the time, he said he wasn't really mad at me, nor did he suspect me of trying to exploit the students, but he never saw the point of my work: "I don't see why a *school* (teacher) should be so interested in my *personal life.*" The idea of what was too personal to write about was central to Kareem's work in my class. In the only interview with him I have on tape, we trail off of a discussion on an individual paper about *The Narrative of the Life of Frederick Douglass* to the more general topic of his recent school performance:

Eli Goldblatt: Let me just ask you a more general question. You haven't been doing a whole lot of writing for this class the last while. Is there a reason for that having to do with the writing? I mean, is it hard to write at all?

Kareem: I don't say it's hard. I don't know what it is.

[*Pause*]

EG: You seem often to say, or at least imply, that you have this idea in your head of what you want to say, but it's very hard to say it. Is that part of what the writing thing is about?

Kareem: Everybody has that.

EG: Well, I know. But you're more pronounced than some others. You hold yourself back more than others in the class do. Can you tell me about that? What is it that's going on there?

Kareem: Going on where?

EG: You know, why is it that you're not turning stuff in. You're not even talking in class as much as you used to.

Kareem: Well, because maybe the class got too, uh, personal.

EG: The class got too personal?

Kareem: Everything that we do now is based on our feelings toward things.

EG: Uh huh. And that feels like it's too . . . does that make it harder to write?

Kareem: Yeah, in some cases, yeah.

EG: Why? You feel like its not . . .

Kareem: See you trying to get into the same thing that what's-her-name was trying to get into.

EG: Jane? [the video artist]. I'm really not I'm maybe—

Kareem: That's what it seems like.

EG: What I'm trying to get into at the very base is you have not produced much work in school in my class in the last two months.

Kareem: You get too personal.

EG: Is that what it is? And what happens when I get too personal?

Kareem: You mean what's the result?

EG: I mean, do you sit down and try to write but it doesn't come out or . . .

Kareem: Yeah, I sit down and try to write, but every assignment you give is based on my feelings towards something.

EG: Is that true for the Fredrick Douglass assignments?

Kareem: No, but I told you I didn't know how you wanted me to do it, but when we got to class and Danny started it off and I was like oh is that what he wanted us to do, just tell what's going on, that's—I knew I could do that.

EG: Well, for instance, you missed what Marie did the other day, and what she did is probably a little closer to what I originally assigned—I mean, I don't mind what you guys were doing today, but—what we were getting at was what were the main ideas underneath it, whereas what you guys were doing was saying what was going on step by step.

Kareem: Like when you asked for a title for the chapter? I couldn't think of a title for the chapter.

EG: Well, Danny said something about that today. That there are a lot of things in it, and they almost seem to be contradicting one another. And one of the things I'm trying to push toward is why Douglass does that. Why he seems to put different things together. And that's why coming up with a title is important. Now, as far as asking you for your personal feelings—I mean, you look at the assignments over the last two months; they haven't been terribly personal except that they are asking from you to come up with an opinion, a personal response, to the material that you're presented. Now is that what you mean?

Kareem: It's the same thing—how you feel about something. I never in all my other classes, you know, they never told me how I feel about something in the assignment. It's not how do you feel You might every once in a while get something like that.

EG: Well, what kind of assignment would you rather have that would be easier for you to do?

Kareem: I can't just answer. I can't answer that question.

EG: Why not?

Kareem: Because, I mean, I just can't. It's not saying something's easy or harder. It's just some things you might not want to answer.

EG: Right, so I'm saying what kind of question would you like to have that would be easier or you would feel more comfortable answering?

[*Pause*]

EG: Or put another way. You did answer this question about how do you see slavery in the eighties. Was that an easier question to answer?

Kareem: I don't know. It's still, it's still dealing with what I feel. Everything we do is dealing with what one's self feels, what one's self sees—what I see, what she sees, you know, that's what this whole class is based on.

I take the liberty to quote this rather lengthy section because it gives the flavor of our talk and demonstrates, too, that the issue for Kareem was not simply trying to keep a nosy white man out of his business or being unable to trust a teacher with his problems. Those explanations would be too easy, too glib.

Assignments that asked him to reshape information along the lines of his own thinking were, for him, "too personal" to respond to. In the end, the whole writing enterprise was "too personal" for Kareem. To venture anything on paper meant to commit himself to positions that could be traced back to his own standing in the world. Despite all he said about being strong and proud, he could not bring himself to venture more than a bare account of events in the public arena of written texts. The above conversation ended in silence, and I had to turn the tape off in the hopes that, without the recorder running, Kareem could answer my questions more comfortably. But he could say no more with the tape off, and, though I ended the interview on my usual note of encouragement and concrete assignments to be handed in soon, I said good-bye to him with a great feeling that I'd failed once again to "get to the bottom" of his silence.

I think now that there was no bottom. He will be silent until he identifies with meaning-making institutions enough so that all questions won't seem so crushingly personal and private. My questions to him *were* personal, in the sense that they requested from Kareem a response that I could not have gotten from anyone else in the class. I was perhaps not prepared for how alone Kareem felt in forming opinions and taking positions. In his imagined battlefield of discourse, it was Kareem against a world whose rules he did not care to understand. Silence felt safer than speech, even if it meant not being very successful in a world in which he wanted to shine.

Neighborhood Paper Drafts

Now I want to turn my attention to a writing project that did not focus on Kareem but on the world around him. During the fall 1988 semester, Kareem wrote a series of three drafts of an essay on his neighborhood, writing in response to the same assignment for which Maria wrote her neighborhood paper. The project came out of class discussions on how each student's neighborhood might differ from others. We had a lecture by the school principal on the history of Philadelphia and the variety of neighborhoods in the city, and we talked about the possibility of collecting all the papers into a booklet. Each student had one class period devoted to the first draft of his or her neighborhood paper and rewrote the paper based on student critiques. The student critiques were excellent, focusing on the issues and topics the drafts brought up but explored incompletely and on the overall structure of each paper. Students were the primary participants of the critique sessions although I was an active participant, especially at the end of the sessions. The third drafts came after I commented on the second drafts turned into me.

Here is the text of Kareem's first draft:

9–26–88

Mount Airy is a fairly nice neighborhood. It is located right next to Germentown and right before Chestnut Hill. I live on the east side of Germentown Ave. and sence Germentown seperates east and west Mount Airy, I live in east Mount Airy.

When you want to talk about th streets, we are practicly the same as any other neighborhood, but Mount Airy dosen't have any gangs. As far as drugs are concerned, the users and abusers are here but the Drugs are not sold around here. If you lived in my neighborhood and you wanted drugs, then you would have to travel a few blocks. You probably wouldn't have to leave Mount Airy completely but you would be leaving my neighborhood.

Unlike alot of other neighborhoods in Philly, there are few buses that travel through Mount Airy. They are the = 23, the, H, the XH, the 18, the L and the Chestnut Hill trains. Out of those buses and trains I mentioned, the H, 23, and the Chestnut Hill east trains are the ones around my way. If you are formillier with those buses, thn you know that they are very convient to get down town.

Overall my neighborhood is very pleasant and clean. I've lived in Mount Airy for 16 years and I've did my share of complaining, but I still enjoy living there

Structurally, this essay is nicely formed into paragraphs. The first paragraph places his neighborhood geographically, the second addresses the issue of drugs, the third describes the public transportation linking his neighborhood with the rest of the city, and the fourth reworks his initial description of Mount Airy as "fairly nice" into "pleasent and clean." As far as I know, Kareem had not specifically been taught the "five paragraph theme," but despite his sloppiness in spelling and proofreading, he did produce a symmetrically shaped essay with an introduction, a conclusion, and a body with two topicalized paragraphs. This indicates that Kareem's "writing problem" was not due to some innate inability to understand standard forms—either grammatical or rhetorical—for he demonstrates here an impressive grasp of tidy formalism. The question for Kareem is what reality he is willing to represent. Although the essay seems unelaborated, fragmented, and contradictory, it does offer the reader a picture of his neighborhood as uncomplicated and coherent, dominated by institutions whose natures, whether evil or good, are unproblematically stable.

The essay begins to answer the question we had discussed in class about the differences between neighborhoods, but without taking on issues that would complicate the job of giving the teacher "what he wants"—a tidy little essay. Kareem is a writer here, but not an author.

He neither draws on the analytical power available to him from classroom subjects like social studies or English, nor does he write as a fully authorized member of his home community, representing in detail the character of Mount Airy. Since he doesn't take on the role of representative either of an academic discipline or a neighborhood formation, he is limited in what he can write. An authority-less author has too little institutional sponsorship even to approach the complex dramas that go on around him. Let me illustrate this point with my own meditation on Kareem's text paragraph by paragraph.

The first paragraph has great meaning if you know northwest Philadelphia. Mount Airy is a racially mixed, predominantly middle-class neighborhood. To the southeast lies Germantown, a neighborhood whose economically mixed population includes more poor people than Mount Airy does. To the northwest lies Chestnut Hill, one of the wealthiest neighborhoods in Philadelphia, also mixed racially but with a higher proportion of whites than either Germantown or Mount Airy. Germantown Avenue runs through the middle of each of these neighborhoods. The avenue acts as a dividing line for Mount Airy, which has separate neighborhood organizations for the east and west side of the road. East Mount Airy is somewhat less well off and more predominantly black.

The neighborhoods Kareem refers to in his first paragraph are assumed elements in a Philadelphian's picture of the city. Chestnut Hill is not merely a place; it is the shining spot at the very top of the long avenue hill. Its name, for most Philadelphians, is a more accurate descriptor than "socialite," "powerful attorney," "old wealth"—these are all mere labels, while "Chestnut Hill" conjures the picture of gray stone houses and tasteful shops. Its businesses, patronized by a clientele more integrated by race than class, are fine without being overpriced: new restaurants, bearing names that sound like film titles; oriental rug and antique dealers, carrying merchandise fit for sultans; book and craft and cheese shops, offering goods no mall store could afford to sell. The groomed homes off the avenue sit on modest parcels of property, and the brief blocks of stucco and brick twins speak of a becoming humility in the neighborhood. But the cobblestones and concrete set around the trolley tracks on the avenue treat traffic gently here, and the people in the venerable old drugstore smile at you even if all you buy is cough drops.

Germantown, on the other hand, brings to mind the bustling corner of Chelton and Germantown avenues, where a street vendor is always burning incense and reading from the Koran over a loudspeaker in front of the boarded-up McDonald's. The local shops sell expensive-looking clothes and electronics cheap. You can buy hamburger and pork chops in bulk from Murray's Steaks, Inc. (keep the plastic bag for the kids to carry school books in), or household supplies from a Russian-Jewish or Korean immigrant who still barely speaks English. The Pennsylvania Dutch candy store still offers handmade chocolates and animal-shaped gumdrops. One block over, the old, abandoned department store building has been taken over by Philadelphia Community College. "Germantown" is all about a neighborhood down on its luck but still kicking—unlike Nicetown, the next "neighb" down the avenue, which has pretty much given itself over to the drugs and decay that want to inch up along the avenue.

Mount Airy sits between these two, sedate compared to its neighbors on either side, more prosperous and promising than one but less secure and in control than the other. Its east side and west side maintain an uneasy peace, held together by common interests but apart by identity clashes. West Mount Airy has a large share of old lefties, medium-level city bureaucrats, and school teachers. East Mount Airy has some of the same but includes more working-class people and a border with a less affluent community. West Mount Airy stands at the edge of Fairmont Park, the city's reminder of William Penn's original woods.

In saying that all of the above is implicit in Kareem's opening paragraph, I am not suggesting that Kareem's language is merely context dependent. It is too simplistic to say that he comes from an oral culture in which his words serve as markers for a concrete reality assumed to be shared by all. I am suggesting, however, that Kareem knows the scene I have just drawn and much more about his neighborhood and the surrounding area. The fact that he is silent on the sociological details is a crucial part of the reality Kareem wishes to represent to himself and others in his writing.

The reality I render in my description of Northwest Philadelphia is one teeming with possibilities, clashes, contradictions. The reality Kareem represents in his opening paragraph is "fairly nice"—there are no rich and poor people, no potholes in the avenue, no crack vials in the playgrounds. The names of the neighborhoods are powerful in the

minds of Philadelphians, but their power is not evoked in a way that
contradicts Kareem's claim for tranquility. His prose leaves the neighborhood unexamined, but it also renders it unproblematic, merely
identifying it by a series of names. This is not just an untrained writer
or a context-dependent narrator; this is a narrator who would rather
not bring to life in writing the complexity with which he lives.

    After all, as a member of the academic community and the middle
class, I have many institutional ways of parsing, classifying, and inter-
preting a complex social scene without being threatened by its contradictions. To speculate on the sociology of Northwest Philadelphia is
not "personal" for me. Kareem, on the other hand, faces the scene
with little institutional machinery to distance himself from the drugs
and rip-offs, the class disparities and racial friction. In fact, the shops
where he buys pizza and clothes, the buses he rides, the druggies he
disdains and fears, *are* among the most important institutional presences in his life that he is consciously aware of manipulating, control-
ling, or resisting. It's not so much that I "know" more; it's that I am
a member of more clubs than Kareem is, especially when it comes to
writing about Mount Airy.

    The next paragraph centers more on an issue that might have chal-
lenged his claim for "niceness," but the language smooths over any
problems the reader might encounter in definition or classification.
First, he claims that "we are practicly the same as any other neighborhood" in relation to the street. He is not consciously lying, but he is
offering a picture of reality that is light-years from his own experience.
The school he went to every day is in a neighborhood practically nothing like Mount Airy. Neighborhood Academy is in the Fairhill area, one
of the most embattled neighborhoods in the city. There are drug dealers on every corner, factories and warehouses in such a state of disrepair
that you cannot tell which are functioning and which are abandoned.
At least four boarded-up rowhouses stand on the block across from the
school, and any kid with a touch of self-preservation knows that crack
and heroin and automatic weapons are written all over the walls of
neighborhood buildings. Kareem could easily have contrasted Mount
Airy with Fairhill and made his neighborhood look as tranquil as a cow
pasture. Why would he start the paragraph saying all neighborhoods
are the same?

    From Kareem's point of view, the reality of "users and abusers" is
the same everywhere. This was a position that I came up against in

many Neighborhood Academy students. I began to see that the assertion was a common sort of defense the kids put up. One student, who lived in the aptly named Nicetown area below Germantown, told me a story about playing football on the street with his younger brother one afternoon when a young woman approached them, put a gun to his brother's head, and demanded to know where a local drug dealer lived. I asked him if this sort of thing scared him enough to make him want to move somewhere else. He told me there was no place he could go where this sort of thing didn't exist—rich neighborhoods or poor all have their crack houses and their drug sellers. This is the attitude toward the problem that Kareem presents by saying his neighborhood is no different than others. There is an implicit acceptance of the nature of "the streets": whether the neighborhood is quiet or rowdy, the workings of illegal money are an institution one lives with. You can't change it, and you are a fool to think you can. All you can do is live around it, and that requires naming it as little as possible.

Kareem does say there are no gangs in Mount Airy and that "Drugs are not sold around here." It's worth noting that when Kareem later wrote a short story based on life in his neighborhood, he wrote about a war between a bad gang—one that dealt drugs and beat people up— and a good gang—one in which the members studied and aspired to college and business careers. I was fascinated by this story because it suggested that no action could be taken without a gang structure to sanction it. The contradiction of a gang promoting success in mainstream culture did lead Kareem into a plot turn where the "good" gang battled the "bad" in a way that made both look reprehensibly violent. In the end, the two gangs were betrayed by a third mediocre and weak gang whose members were waiting for a chance to get rid of both rivals. Though gangs were not a major part of his life in Mount Airy, for Kareem they remained a powerful metaphor for the social organizations of his peers. He was not consciously commenting on his social milieu with his story, which for him was "just a story." In fact, he was a bit shaken up by our class discussion of its meanings, and he never did write the expanded version we recommended. Still, his story suggested the extent to which the mythology of gangs shapes the experience of urban kids growing up even on Mount Airy's peaceful streets.

Kareem pulls a curious rhetorical trick at the end of paragraph two in order to keep the drug deals out of his "neighborhood." He switches the geographical definition of his neighborhood to include only the few blocks immediately around his house (this tighter ring around one's house is usually called "'round my way" by Philadelphia students). As far as drug trafficking is concerned, Mount Airy is no longer Kareem's neighborhood at the end of paragraph two. Kareem thus manages to have it both ways in his drug paragraph, and he pulls off this trick by looking rhetorically naive. He maintains the convenient position that drugs are everywhere and that the best you can do is live peaceably with the "users and abusers." At the same time, he claims that his neighborhood is free of drug dealing and the attendant violence (never mind the account of Jeff thrown through the McDonald's window). I would not argue that Kareem is aware of the slipperiness of his presentation, but I would maintain that his seemingly blunted prose allows him to represent a reality that neither challenges him to change his ways nor presents to the reader an unflattering picture of his home community. This is about as close as he comes to being a representative of his neighborhood, but it is a kind of representation by negation or silence. As awkward as Kareem's writing might be, however, it does the job he wants it to do in avoiding complexity or unpleasant reality.

Before we leave the drug paragraph, I want to comment further on Kareem as a representative of social institutions. Notice the advent of "you" as a rhetorical strategy in this paragraph. In the first paragraph, he had been able to render the geography with simple sentences "Mt. Airy is . . ." and "I live . . ." Now, however, the discourse becomes a dialogue with an interlocutor who is interrogating the narrator. He begins the paragraph "When you want to talk about the streets," as though the reader had specifically asked about "streets," euphemistically meaning the drug trade. The "you" is an outsider, curious enough to ask about where to buy drugs: "If you lived in my neighborhood" (the "you" obviously does not) "and wanted drugs" (but of course the "you" wouldn't want such a thing). At the same time, the "you" is moral enough to approve of a neighborhood which has no gangs and has no drug sellers on the corners.

Kareem is not just writing for a teacher; he is writing for the social system the teacher represents. The system disapproves of gangs and violence and drugs, all of which are marks that a young man would rather not have on his neighborhood. The system fosters the notion that inquiring after the causes of problems will help solve them. He must talk about "the streets" because the teacher expects him to mention street action in a description of a city neighborhood. But he is merely on the defensive here; he does not identify enough with the academy to use school analysis in service of his writing. He derives no authority from his role as a student writing a paper—writing is merely a chore to discharge. Meanwhile, as a representative of his neighborhood, and as an aspiring candidate for entrance into the judgmental middle-class world, the less he says about "the streets" the better. At this point in Kareem's life, he identifies more with the neighborhood than the school world, represents "'round my way" more than the teacher's "way." Yet to represent the world he knows in the neighborhood may jeopardize his standing as an aspiring college-bound student with a possible military career ahead and may possibly besmirch the reputation of his neighborhood as well. He is therefore in a bind from which only vague and contradictory prose can extract him.

The more stories he tells and the more he reveals about what he has seen, the more he calls into existence a reality which he would just as soon ignore. It is my experience that many kids who grow up with far more violence than Kareem ever saw often say quite honestly that they know little or nothing about the street scene. For one thing, their mothers and fathers lock them up at home much of the time, and for another, one needs to cultivate a certain type of ignorance in order to survive. In Kareem's case, the street is not nearly as severe a setting as it is in Fairhill, but he does as little as he can in this paper to bring it into his school life, even though it is knowledge expressly requested by the teacher. He seems to be operating under the principle that whatever he doesn't name just won't be there.

The paragraph that follows in his first draft is one of my favorite writing moments in the entire school year. Kareem recites for us the letters and numbers of the public transportation routes, omitting until the end any mention of where these routes lead. Here is naming with a vengeance, bringing into existence a system with no fare hikes, breakdowns, or attendant crime but a heck of a lot of track, equipment, and overhead cable. I once knew a hippie traveler who had ridden all over the country on boxcars, hardly ever venturing out of the freight yards. He was a quiet guy who never bragged about his exploits or even told stories about the people he'd met riding the rails. All he had to show for his travels was a secret notebook, which he only showed his closest friends. In it, he had recorded the numbers of engines he had seen over the years. The numbers seemed to conjure for him the reality he wanted to see—a system more or less untroubled by labor disputes or financial woes or historical injustices—one that he had both constructed for himself and experienced as verifiably real.

In his paragraph, Kareem demonstrates his knowledge of the system and substantiates the claim that his neighborhood is well served by merely listing the lines Mount Airy people could ride. The fact of those numbers and letters on the page is comforting and unproblematic, real and yet nonthreatening. The explanation that all these lines are "very convient to get down town" is an afterthought which I will consider in a moment.

There is a striking parallel between the opening sentence of this paragraph and the opening of the preceding one. He asserts earlier that his neighborhood is *like* other neighborhoods "when you want to talk about the streets," but now he claims it is *unlike* other neighborhoods in the number of buses that "travel through Mount Airy." Since Kareem's prose is chronically error-ridden, it is hard to be certain how to read "there are few busses," but, if you assume he left out an "a," he probably means that most neighborhoods only have one or two bus routes while Mount Airy has "a few." Since he goes on to list routes, I interpret the sentence as emphasizing, with modest understatement, how many buses Mount Airy residents have at their disposal. This is a bit of local pride that many Mount Airy residents will express. I recently did an informal poll asking Mount Airy friends what they thought of SEPTA service in their neighborhood, and they all agreed that Mount Airy has more access to transportation than most other neighborhoods. But why is it so important to Kareem to be able to leave his part of town?

One answer is that, as I showed in the section on Kareem's personal writing, shopping makes him feel as if he is part of the culture. He can get to the malls and shopping centers, which give him a sense that he matters, on these buses. Moreover, the system itself is one globalizing institution that Kareem knows and identifies with, and the fact that the lines reach his house is an indication that his part of the world is connected, that traffic to and from Mount Airy is important enough to warrant four buses, two trains (named for the wealthy neighborhood up the avenue), and a trolley.

When he first turned the paper in to me, I saw the focus on SEPTA as a metaphor for "getting somewhere" in the world, but the more I look at the paragraph and Kareem's journal the more convinced I become that the focus here is on the esoteric substance of the system itself, which you must be "formillier with" (that spelling is so elaborate, as if it required a knowledge of French to understand how the buses run) in order even to understand SEPTA's convenience.

For the record, only the more expensive trains lead directly downtown; other public routes require a sizable ride and two transfers to get to the main Center City mall. Their "convenience" is apparent only to an experienced as well as a knowledgeable traveler—compared to walking or trying to park, I suppose SEPTA buses and subways are models of convenience. I know a Guatemalan immigrant who rode the 23 trolley for months without transferring to the much faster subway because the idea of braving the crowds, knowing how to negotiate transfers, and being able to get off at the right stop was too much for her. Most suburban Philadelphians would feel the same.

In this paragraph, Kareem has taken over as the teacher in the dialogue. Whereas in the last paragraph the "you" was asking the questions, here he makes the lists in a straightforward syntax, and he only mentions a "you" to challenge us about whether or not we are SEPTA cognoscenti. Thus, one of the virtues of Kareem's neighborhood is that it has opened the way for him to learn the system. And, given his knowledge, he can write a solid paragraph without having to introduce into written reality any elements which are contradictory, puzzling, or difficult to face. The facts stand neatly as the facts. He need not mention the obvious class distinction between the $3.00, twenty-minute ride on the Chestnut Hill local that lawyers and bureaucrats take in the morning and the $1.75, hour-long ride on the bus and subway that workers and people on the way to court take.

I would not expect Kareem to develop a sophisticated critique of the public transit system. In a strange way, what I might expect is far more disorganized, fragmented writing. The question is not why Kareem writes "poorly"; the question is why does he write so "well"? His writing could easily be torn with conflicting impulses, filled with contradictory details. Instead, what he chooses to represent is a monolithic system symbolized by a set of letters and numbers. By giving us this list of route names to stand for the system, Kareem represents the system as seamless and acts as a representative of a social institution much less threatening to him than the school system, the police, or the drug underground. In the process, he locates himself for other Philadelphians and establishes his neighborhood as a nexus of communicating lines.

The final paragraph is short but revealing. Now his neighborhood is "pleasant and clean." He has said nothing to substantiate this claim, and a writing teacher is paid to call a student on such an undefended position. "But really," Kareem might object, "this is just an extension of 'nice.' After all, I'm not *claiming* as much as I am adding adjectives to the overall description." I might accept this—Mount Airy *is* clean and pleasant compared to most parts of the city—except for one detail. He suggests in the final paragraph that he has complained about Mount Airy in the past, but he gives us no indication what might have troubled him about his neighborhood.

Kareem invokes his sixteen years in Mount Airy as authority for the claims in the paper, and presumably his "share of complaining" also justifies his opinion that "I still enjoy living there." The neatness of the package makes me feel that "pleasant and clean" applies more to the representation in the paper than to the streets of Mount Airy. Everything is tied up just so and, although the complaints alluded to are left unspoken, the orderly paragraphs have "dealt with" the subject (I once had a student inform me, when I suggested that he needed biology to fill out his roster, that he had "dealt with biology" in a previous school) and modeled for us a reality that Kareem would like us to understand is his. In short, Kareem's sixteen years in Mount Airy haven't conferred the neighborhood's authority on him because he is unwilling to represent the neighborhood. He is too busy warding off any representation of reality that would undermine the neatness of his writing. Becoming an author requires a weighty responsibility to the sponsoring institution, and Kareem does not identify enough with any institution at this point to take on that burden.

Neighborhood Paper: Second Draft

According to his journal, Kareem was worried on the day we were to critique his paper. Just before we began the critique, he wrote: "I got on to other students cases, so know its my turn. I suppose the saying

'What goes around come around' " (Oct. 13, 1988). Like most students facing the first critical session focused on them, Kareem was justifiably scared, and although he didn't show it in class, he was a bit belligerent too, for he went on in the entry: "Anyway I'm just gona say what I have to say and the Hell with the other students if they want to talk about me." Yet Kareem had gone to some lengths to say nothing particularly controversial, nothing that could be open to major disagreement. I think what he enjoyed about critiquing other peoples' work was the unraveling that took place when we "got on their case," but it was just that unraveling that he wished wouldn't "come around" to him. Like all of us, he wanted the reality he'd represented to remain intact.

We did, in fact, point out to him issues he had raised but not explored, as well as issues he hadn't raised that we wanted to know more about. It was still early in the school year, and he must have taken our criticism as a challenge, for he put some effort into his revision. Here is the second draft:

10–20–88

Mount Airy

Mount Airy is a fairly nice neighborhood. The reason I say fairly is because we have our ups and downs. Such as people standing on the corner smoking and drinking, only thats just accational. People robbing other peoples belonging and alittle bit of trash here and there. On the other hand, Mount Airy has many, many Good qualities to such as lovely homes, clean streets and parks, recreational activities such as football in the winter and basketball, and baseball in the summer. We have nice businesses such as the VEDIO LIBRARY, The Orange Blosom, the state store and various pizza shops. My personal favorate is the Golden Crust, because of there large stakes.

Although Mount Airy isn't a large neighborhood, It still has a very nice size. It is more or less looser and open then tight and over crowded. We have an East side, West Side, Top Side and Botton side to our neighborhood. Germentown Ave. seperates east and west Mount Airy and because I live on the east side of Germentown ave. I live in east Mount Airy. It isn't dificult at all to get to my neighborhood especialy from center city. You could

take the R.7. Train and get off at Sedgwick, you could take the
Broad-street subway and get off at Erie or Olony. If you get of at
Erie you can take the 23, H, or XH and get off at Germentown
and Mount Pleasent ave. If you go to Oleny you could take the
18 to Spregue and Vernon Rd. or the L to Stenton and Mount
Airy Ave. My house is on the two hundred block of Sydney St.
    In order to get to my neighborhood form city Hall you must
first pass Germentown, which is the neighborhood before mines.
Which is also the drug stop for the drugies around my way. The
reason they go to germentown to get there drugs is because there
are no druges sold around my way. People have tried before to
sell drugs but due to the power of the community and the strengh
of the Police there plans are always foiled.
    Over all my neighborhood is very pleasant and clean. I've live
in Mount Airy for sixteen years and I've did my share of complaining and what goes on such as the trash the corner people and the
drugies. But I still rather live here than any ran down slum pit.

The new draft is formed from a fascinating mixture of internalized
dialogue, merged paragraphs, and telling details bursting out sideways
from the tidy structure of the first version. The opening paragraph is
essentially a gloss on the first sentence, one of only a few sentences to
remain intact from the original draft. The second paragraph combines
and embellishes the geographical information from the original paragraph one and the transit data from the original paragraph three. Paragraph three in this version handles the drug issue from a very different
perspective than the one presented in the first draft. The fourth and
concluding paragraph is an elaborate rewrite of the original conclusion,
spiced with more details and stronger language. The whole is richer in
local color and expression, less tight-lipped, although here too the overarching intention seems to be to represent a neighborhood whose problems and contradictions are basically under control.
    In the first paragraph, the reader can almost hear the imagined
questions Kareem is responding to:

    Critic: What do you mean by "fairly nice"?
    Kareem: The reason I say "fairly" is because we have our ups
    and downs.

Critic: Such as?
Kareem: Such as people standing on the corner and smoking and drinking [raised eyebrows of the critics], only that's just occasional.
Critic: Anything else?
Kareem: People robbing other people's belongings and a little bit of trash here and there.
Critic: Sounds messed up.
Kareem: On the other hand, . . .

The implicit dialogue explains the appearance of fragments in this revision, where there had been none in the original. It also explains how he could get so far afield in the first paragraph that he ends by telling you his favorite pizza shop. As any of us might in the heat of an interview, he becomes so concerned to answer the questions that he loses track of his own purpose; he abdicates his authority to the imagined critical readers. This leaves him little to pick up on when he starts paragraph two, but he has, at least, managed to represent Mount Airy recreational and business life in his text with the digression. Readers may not know where Mount Airy is or who lives there, but we know people can play ball, rent videos, buy liquor and pizza and Philadelphia cheese steaks there. A fairly nice neighborhood indeed.

After the relative specificity of the last two sentences in the opening paragraph, the first half of the second paragraph appears vague and pointless. It is devoted to expanding the geographical information Kareem originally presented, but, although he tries to say more, he succeeds in meaning less. The opening sentence takes on the question of relative size without having anything else to compare the neighborhood to, leaving him to assert inconsequentially that Mount Airy is not large but "a very nice size." In the following sentence, "It is more or less looser and open then tight and over crowded" (which sounds so much like the kind of explanation and analysis Kareem often used in class) only leads him further into nonstatement. He is trying to suggest a palpable metaphor, an evocation of city landscape as fabric, and does give a feeling to the distinction he wants to make between Mount Airy and more densely populated neighborhoods. But he knows the metaphor is undeveloped and that his critics will respond to it with quizzical looks. He therefore follows up the abstract "loose and open" description with a concrete name for each side of the neighborhoods. Since the names tell us nothing about the character of the place, however, this sentence fails to clarify what his metaphor has clouded. He merely succeeds in boxing up the space and looking a little silly in the process. Returning almost in desperation to a sentence that worked for him last time, he divides Mount Airy in two and places himself on the east.

My guess is that Kareem includes his SEPTA section in this paragraph because the geographical information doesn't control the terrain well enough. Where geography had been prominent—if conveniently abbreviated—in the last draft, here it is demoted to the second paragraph following an introduction that opens a Pandora's box of details. He is more ambitious this time with the description of geography, attacking the size and texture of the neighborhood, but at this point he has only succeeded in becoming more abstract and vague. The definitive boundaries of Mount Airy remain unsurveyed by language after nearly a page; he needs a boost from incoming traffic.

In the first version, Kareem justified SEPTA's appearance because buses "travel through Mt. Airy" and the transit system made it convenient "to get down town." In this version, the focus is on how "to get to my neighborhood especially from center city." He no longer takes the reader's knowledge for granted but instead offers easy directions to bring the reader within a block of his house. I suspect he hadn't meant to lead the readers to his doorstep—otherwise the paragraph would have given a clue of this intention earlier, or at the very least he would have given us the exact address (as Maria did in the second draft of her neighborhood paper)—but, having gotten us on the bus, he had to provide us a stop to get off, and his street was the most convenient destination.

The inclusion of Kareem's street name represents a problem the second draft shares with the previous version. As I pointed out earlier, Kareem was quite willing to redefine his neighborhood when he wanted to proscribe undesirables from his territory. In neither of the first two drafts does he really identify with his neighborhood as a whole; his own home is still very much the center of things. Even when he mentions in this draft the shops of Mount Airy, he does not present them as part of a business district with a character distinct from Germantown and Chestnut Hill. He sees those shops in terms of what he and his friends like to consume. For Kareem, "neighborhood" is where a person lives rather than an institution one can step back from and investigate. Although writing requires both some detachment and some identification with an institution greater than self and home, Kareem resists taking a step closer or farther from his subject. It is not until the third draft that he develops a position as a writer that allows him to organize his information rather than be organized by it, and to approximate a consistent position of authority as the author of his text. As we will see, something is lost as well as gained in that development.

If there was any doubt that Kareem was capable of more sophisticated writing, the opening of paragraph three lays it to rest. "In oder to get to my neighborhood form city Hall you must first pass Germentown" is a clever transition from the previous paragraph about travel to the next paragraph about drugs. Notice that in his description of travel he never directs us to get off the bus or trolley in Germantown. We have merely passed through it, and the transition depends upon recalling to us the neighborhood we saw out the window along the way.

Any city math teacher will recognize such surprising revelations of skill in students: a kid who does not know his or her multiplication tables will frequently invent methods that are mathematically more sophisticated to get around the deficiency. You find students who have devised abacuslike counting systems to figure the product of 7 x 8 by addition. In the same way, Kareem has had to produce a brilliant transition to make up for the fact that paragraph two and paragraph three are neither in a logical order nor do they contribute to a coherently conceived portrait of Mount Airy. The fact that he cares to make the transition, and that he recognizes it is needed, indicates that he knows a good deal about what readers need from writers and what teachers expect from students. He is perfectly capable of producing crucial rhetorical effects.

Better than any other moment in the writing I've reviewed so far, this transition gives us a glimpse of Kareem's potential and reinforces the point I have been making. Kareem does not lack "skills" primarily. His relationship to institutionally shaped reality, such as urban geography and public transit systems and political power, is so different from the relationship we expect an "author" to have that the texts he produces must seem skewed and peculiar to our eyes.

The following two *which*-clauses act like two cars needing to be parked in one garage space. The one Kareem chooses to install inside the sentence boundaries, "which is the neighborhood before mines," was probably the logical choice because of the revisions he has made. In the previous draft we were introduced to Germantown at the outset, but in this draft that information has been excised from the geography lesson, so Kareem must go back and identify Germantown before he can comment on it. The second clause, the one that actually carries the main topic of the paragraph, is thus left to stand on its own—paradoxically both a topic sentence and a fragment. Perhaps it is the very importance of the clause that leads Kareem to believe it can stand alone, particularly after the fancy footwork of the opening transition.

The paragraph itself is really always in transition, never focusing on one point for more than a clause. Although "drugs" is the general topic, Kareem dances around the issue, touching related topics along the way and rolling free of it all without ever having to linger on any one point. Here is a synopsis of the assertions in paragraph three:

1. To get to Mount Airy, you must pass Germantown.
2. Germantown is the neighborhood before Mount Airy.
3. Germantown is the drug stop for druggies in my near neighborhood. (Notice that this subsumes the admission in the earlier draft that Mount Airy does have its "users and abusers," but it cleverly deemphasizes the admission.)
4. No drugs are sold in my near neighborhood.
5. People tried to sell drugs in my neighborhood in the past.
6. Two forces foiled drug sales: community power and police strength.

Any one of these assertions could serve as a topic sentence for a separate paragraph. In fact, the six statements could serve as an outline for a well-organized high school paper on the drug problem in Mount Airy. Once again, it would be easy to dismiss the sketchiness here as a result of Kareem's "poor" writing skills. Yet, how well this sketchiness serves an underlying purpose! By not elaborating on any of these assertions, Kareem avoids representing a problem which, in its complexity and intransigence, would not only challenge his main thesis that Mount Airy is a "fairly nice" neighborhood, but also would force Kareem to confront a reality fraught with choices to make and dangers to avoid. The elliptical version he presents, complete with a comforting show of adult force that makes the evil go away, tells the story he is willing at this point to enter into the public record.

In the drug paragraph, Kareem is still reacting to questions by his critic-readers. The extra *which*-clause can be read as an additional bit of information elicited by the puzzled face of his interlocutor. The phrase "The reason they go to germentown" also has the sound of a response to the question "Why do they have to go to Germantown?" Yet in this paragraph, Kareem is acting like a cagey interviewee trying hard to control the situation—rather like the way he must have acted with the admissions officer at Kutztown when they interpreted his guarded answers as disinterest—for he does not want to reveal to us or to himself the extent of his knowledge and experience. He is not trying to hide from the accusation of being a druggie himself. Were that the case he might have spent more time distancing himself from those he knew in the drug trade or simply have avoided the topic entirely. Instead, he hides from the problematic reality that a more detailed representation would bring to life.

Unfortunately, in order to suppress that outside reality, he must come off as more aloof and incurious than he is. I believe this almost reflexive denial led to a poor impression at interviews and low grades in school, both of which encouraged him to remain silent, to take even fewer risks in the way he presented himself and his home surroundings.

As with the other paragraphs, Kareem revised the final paragraph of this draft along the lines of the questions critical readers might ask. He made two substantive changes. First, he added the phrase "and what goes on such as the trash the corner people and the drugies." In an orderly and standard high school theme, this phrase in the concluding paragraph would be used to recall the details in the paragraphs devoted to trash, corner people, and druggies. In the present paper, however, it gives the reader an idea of those problems largely left out of the representation. It is a bow to a reality not evoked here, and at the same time it relegates those problems to the category of insignificant irritations.

The second addition gives an even more shocking glimpse into the reality denied a name in this paper. By substituting the vehement assertion "But I still rather live here than any ran down slum pit" for the original innocuous closing clause, "but I still enjoy living there," Kareem elevates into visibility the comparison implicit in a discussion of any neighborhood. Rather than claiming his neighborhood is "practicly the same as any other neighborhood," as he did in the first draft, now

Kareem closes his essay with a slur on other parts of the city. The drug paragraph had come close to making an open comparison between Germantown and Mount Airy—*they* allow drugs but *we* do not—but he said nothing there explicitly to condemn another community. He makes no effort here to show what a "ran down slum pit" looks like in comparison with his own tree-lined street, but the language he uses is enough to indicate that other, unnamed, neighborhoods deserve his contempt while his neighborhood only occasionally earns his complaint. Perhaps his silence on the "slum pits" was an unconscious way of avoiding offense to others in the class—there were some in the group who really did live in neighborhoods much rougher and more broken down than Mount Airy—but the violence of this final shot reveals strong feelings that are otherwise not expressed in the paper.

Neighborhood Paper: Third Draft

The day Kareem turned in his third and final version of the neighborhood paper, he wrote the following entry in his journal:

> Yesterday I made yet another copy of my neighborhood. If it's not good enough this time, then what can I say or do. I should have done my homework after I finished it but I was dead tired, so all I did was go to sleep. Today I am bored as hell with nothing to talk about and no one to talk to. It makes me very depressed being like this. I know that everyone expects too much from me, and I just can't forfill everyone wishes and desires. So either take me as I am or don't take me at all. The only thing I am looking forward to is tomorrow's pay. (Nov. 3, 1988)

Let me point out, before I say anything about the content, that this entry makes clear that Kareem was perfectly capable of using a construction like "I should have done" in standard English form, so that the expression "I've did my share of complaining," which he used in the first two neighborhood paper drafts, was not merely a result of his "ignorance" of standard dialect. It may in part have been a register cue—he wanted his paper ending to have a colloquial feel to it—or, more likely, he just didn't care to pay attention to such details about the product. I cannot prove this in any scientific way, but I have the general impression that Kareem committed more "grammar" errors in his assigned papers than he did in his journal. There may be many explanations for that, since formal papers require more grappling with public discourse. In any case, I would argue that on the whole Kareem's seeming "ignorance" of standard usage was more often the result of a tendency to *ignore* school language rather than the demonstration of incomplete knowledge about it. One might almost call it passive-aggressive behavior in the face of standard English and the institutions that ask for it. When one considers the consequences for more overt aggression toward institutions, passive-aggressive behavior can be an attractive option.

The conflation of revising a paper about his neighborhood and making "yet another copy of my neighborhood" is more than a curious slip. As the reader will readily see, the third draft is a substantial revision of the earlier versions, yet this entry suggests Kareem sees his rewrite as a "copy," perhaps because it is still fulfilling the same assignment. It does represent a new "copy" of his neighborhood, if that word can be interpreted to mean an alternative representation, or model, of the area he knows so well. The expression may even suggest something of the way Kareem sees written language operating: for him, writing produces copies of reality that are less vital and interesting, and certainly more irritating, than the "real thing." In this theory of writing, Kareem is hardly alone. At the very least, most of us are Platonists in high school.

In the above journal entry, Kareem's attitude about his third draft is not hopeful. He seems to expect that it will not be well received, and he is preparing for rejection by adopting stances of belligerent despair ("what can I say or do") and then listless withdrawal ("I was dead tired, so all I did was go to sleep [remember his reaction to the news of the birth of his son]. Today I am bored as hell with nothing to talk about and no one to talk to"). He does see that what he feels is a condition he doesn't like, and his comment that "It makes me very depressed being like this" sounds very like a call for help from me, the reader of his journal. But he goes on to put more distance between himself and those who might look for something from him with the remark "So either take me as I am or don't take me at all." That is a challenge to go beyond the grading relationship and offer unconditional love and support—something I think Kareem needed almost as much as he needed guidance and critical attention—yet it is offered in a tone that suggests he is looking for an excuse to call the writing and revision process off as so much futile effort for an unsatisfiable master.

For me, his final remark that "the only thing I am looking forward to is tomorrows pay" casts the writing situation in a cold economic light. I know it probably refers to his after-school job—Kareem worked sometimes all night cleaning supermarket floors in New Jersey, so he told me—but I also read this as a comment on the teacher-student relationship developed by my emphasis on drafts. It sounds like he is wishing that he could return to a model of the student-teacher relationship in which being a student was a simple, if more menial, job with a grade in your envelope at the end of the pay period. Doing multiple drafts forces Kareem out of that neat economic relationship under which he has no responsibility for the assignment or the product (with little hope for a pay raise), and into a more complex relationship where what you get depends on how you yourself conceive of the job. One can see this as the distinction between the most despairing image of a job as dependable servitude and the most idealistic version of the middle-class work ethic. I would be wary of such a neat polarization, but there is no doubt that Kareem's November 3, 1988, entry expresses little optimism for how he'll profit from all his brainwork. This was perhaps the clearest articulation of his desire to do well in my class, but characteristically it comes in the form of a challenge to reject him and a threat that he will withdraw if I do.

Here is the final version of Kareem's neighborhood paper:

11–2–88

Mt. Airy

My neighborhood is Mount Airy. Mount Airy is located above the Germantown section of Philadelphia. It is found right above Germantown and right Below Chestnut Hill.

If you were to come to my neighborhood looking for good and nice neighbors, then you would have come to the right place. There are mostly blacks and whites live in my neighborhood, but we also have Chinese and Hispanics too, and we all get along with each other.

The community works very hard in keeping our street clean and safe. We have a 24 hour town watch and it seems to be working just fine. In the past few years, the crime rate has dropped tremendously.

Just a few years ago, in my eyes, Mount Airy was headed for a down fall. It seemed like the teenage kids were the cause of every problem from burglary and auto theft, to gang wars and drug abuse. It seemed like, there was no stopping them.

I remember seeing a few teenage kids hanging at the train station just waiting for their turn to either steal a car or snatch purses from ladies when they got off of the trains. I also saw a few of their plans back-fire, and if they were arrested, they would be back on the streets in two days. It just didn't seem right.

I guess when the neighbor saw that the police were not helping, they decided to take matters into their own hand by starting a strong town watch. Since then my neighborhood has been almost totaly peaceful.

Mount Airy is full of stores and pizza shops, Most which are up on the Ave. Germantown Ave. is the busiest Ave. in the neighborhood. The 23 trolly runs there, the best pizza shops are there and my video club is on the Ave. too.

.It isn't difficult at all to get to my neighborhood, especialy from Center City. You could take the R.7. train and get off at Sedgwick, you could take the Broad Street subway and get off at Erie or Olney. If you get off at Erie, you could take the 23, H, or XH buses and get off at Germantown and Mount Pleasant Ave. If you go to Olney, you could take the 18 to Sprague and Vernon Road or the L to Stenton and Mount Airy Ave. My house is on the two hundred block of Sydney Street

I like Mt. Airy for its clean st., lovely homes, and kind neighbors. Maybe that why I like living here so much.

This version is a good deal more than another "copy" of his earlier drafts. The second draft was more than double the length of the first draft, but operated with roughly the same organizational structure. This draft is only a dozen or so words longer than the second draft, but its focus, narrator, and rhetorical strategy are all changed. Even the number of mechanical mistakes has been reduced noticeably. Although it still lacks some of the qualities a standard high school essay is usually expected to have (for instance, there is still no clear statement of thesis in the first paragraph), I would venture to say that, formally, Kareem's third draft would not stand out as sketchy or incomplete in a majority of English classrooms in American high schools throughout the country. It does not reveal a tremendous amount about his neighborhood, but it indicates, particularly in the section about crime, that his neighborhood has a definite story that is worth telling and listening to.

In this version he seems to focus on the ability of his community to work together. After an opening paragraph that surveys the geography as simply as his first version did, he introduces the neighborliness of the community. This sets up the reader for the next four paragraphs, in which the drama of Mount Airy is presented: crime—particularly teenage crime—grew and then was defeated by the strength of neighbors working together. There follows a shortened version of his second draft's opening, the paragraph that sketches in the good qualities of local business from the point of view of a teenager. Then Kareem gives us a more refined version of his SEPTA paragraph, now in the service of a concluding section emphasizing what is good about the neighborhood. When he comes finally to his abbreviated ending, the phrase "clean st., lovely homes, and kind neighbors" does operate to reinforce a theme he has worked hard to present convincingly. He has portrayed Mount Airy as a friendly, thriving business community, willing to protect itself from internal decay and linked effectively to the rest of the city. The whole essay seems to answer the implicit question with which he ends: Why do I like to live here?

The narrator of this version is much more consistent and assertive in organizing material, interjecting opinions, and guiding the reader from place to place. For the first time, Kareem opens with an assertion that "My neighborhood is Mount Airy," as if he now is able to claim his territory explicitly since he has more control of it on paper. He then makes Mount Airy the subject of the next two sentences, highlighting the place rather than his personal involvement in it because he has already asserted his own claim on it unambiguously. "It is found" is a construction that suggests the reader might be looking for Mount Airy; the narrator is happy to oblige with directions. He anticipates the reader's needs rather than responding to questions about statements he has already made.

The "you" of the first sentence of the second paragraph is now a positive persona, "looking for good and nice neighbors," rather than the moralistic voyeur of the first version who wanted to see where drugs were sold. This allows Kareem to isolate the drug and crime issue as an evil that he himself watched and shook his head over ("It just didn't seem right"). He has made an ally of the good-hearted reader and so can introduce his own persona as observer: "in my eyes," "it seemed . . . it seemed," "I remember," "I also saw," "I guess." He uses "we" liberally enough in the beginning paragraphs that when later he refers to the teenage criminals as "them" and then refers to the adults who set up the town watch also in the third person, the effect is touching rather than confusing or distancing. He presents himself as an innocent witness, young enough to have been only a mute observer to the teenage crime wave and the adult response. Here he has used his penchant for seeing events as happening *to* him in the best possible rhetorical way by telling a story in which that position is both appropriate and affecting.

The closing paragraphs on Mount Airy shops and SEPTA connections are not as sharply motivated as the previous paragraphs, but both of them serve a purpose for the whole that was far less apparent in the earlier drafts. The shops section in the second draft had derailed the paper at the beginning, while the SEPTA section in both earlier versions had been almost a comical interlude, leading readers on a ride but never explaining why. In this version, they have both been demoted to the latter half of the paper after the major story has been told, and in this position they serve well to flesh out the life and location of Kareem's neighborhood.

The lack of direct assertion in this section leaves Kareem little to say in the final paragraph, although he may simply have run out of energy by the end of yet another "copy" of his neighborhood. As with the crime and neighborhood life sections, the ending sentence is cheerful, giving the whole a feeling of the upbeat prose in a junior chamber of commerce pamphlet. Having left out his claim that Mount Airy is "fairly nice," he has done more in this draft to argue just that.

Still, when I look back at the three drafts, I feel that a special character of the other two versions was lost in the more polished third. The last draft presents Mount Airy confidently, posits a narrator who has seen events go from bad to better, and presents a picture of the neighborhood as integrated, pretty, and well-connected. The earlier drafts are disorganized, fragmented by a dialogue with outside critics that never allows the prose to settle into whole sentences building one upon

another. But the earlier drafts also contain hints of complexity and conflict, of problems the author would just as soon not name. I would not
say that, as a writing teacher, I am not pleased with the "progress"
Kareem made in his three drafts. Indeed, I was overjoyed with the last
version and willing to call it his "final" rewrite. But, as a close reader
of his texts, I am both fascinated and disconcerted by the course of
development in authority that his drafts reveal.

Conclusion

The neighborhood paper was probably Kareem's last, best effort in the
1988–89 school year. Soon after the Christmas break, he started pulling
away from school, and he never again put out the kind of work I had
seen from him in October. I don't believe he lacked encouragement at
school, nor do I think there was a specific problem at home. Throughout that semester, I did what I could to motivate him again and to help
him find a college he could look forward to attending the following
year. Kareem had no acceptances in hand at the time he graduated, but
I met him on the street in Mount Airy at the end of the summer and
he had already finished a summer session at a traditionally black college
in the South to which a friend of his had always been urging him to apply. In 1993 he was still in college, and I have some hope that he may
have begun to tap the intelligence and energy I always knew he had.

I think the one rule that emerges from the study of Kareem's writing is that as an author he chooses to name—and thus bring into existence—only those aspects of reality which his prose can control. He
is on the most solid ground with his account of the SEPTA connections
to Mount Airy, and this may explain why it is the only section that
appears substantially in all three drafts. But the rule holds well for all
the writing I have reviewed. Whether it is in his private retelling of a
shopping jaunt or his public version of drugs in his neighborhood,
Kareem represents systems of buying and selling as relatively unproblematic and stable. He seems to want to convey the impression that
nothing in his world is particularly jarring or surprising, and even the
evil is a manageable, normal part of everyday reality.

The paradox in this approach is that in order to seem in control of
reality by selectively naming its parts, he forces himself into the position

of being passive in relation to events. The way Kareem lists people, occurrences, stores, or merchandise gives him the appearance of dominating objective facts, while his avoidance of underlying causes—the history of conflicts, the feelings that motivate his and others' actions—protects him from seeming confused or overwhelmed by a world of contradictory forces. By focusing so much on only those qualities he can enumerate, he unwittingly portrays himself as a victim, a consumer, a petitioner dependent on luck and the good will of greater powers.

In short, Kareem makes the choice to be silent rather than "personal." He wants to represent himself, and his neighborhood, as strong and controlled, and to do that he must omit mention of anything that might suggest weakness, vulnerability, distress. He must not represent, to himself or to his reader, any sign of caring for the son he fathered but cannot raise or provide for. He cannot afford to say about his third draft: "This is great. I think you'll like it." He cannot even ask for advice on how to pass a course or apply to college, although no admissions officer in the world could convince me that Kareem didn't want to succeed in just those ways.

The only place Kareem reveals dangerous material in a sustained way is in the third draft of his neighborhood paper. There he gives the reader at least two unabashed paragraphs in which he reports on crime in his neighborhood. He describes people doing things he regards as wrong, and he admits he does not know what to do about it ("It seemed like, there was no stopping them"). He is willing to sustain a longer exposition of questionable events, without trying to answer those who might be critical of his neighborhood for what he describes, because he knows that the ending will suit the imagined reader's desire for good to triumph over evil. He can take the problem on in his prose because he identifies with the institution that he believes can solve the problem.

Up until the third draft, Kareem was trying to represent his neighborhood without having a clear sense of who he was as a representative. He didn't fully see himself as a representative of Mount Airy, for he was willing to shift the boundaries of his "neighborhood" to keep drug dealers away from his turf. He pictured businesses from the point of view of what they sold him and his friends, not as constituting elements in a community sphere greater than his circle of friends. But, at the same time, he could not write as a member of an overarching and sponsoring discipline like sociology or literature—institutions that would have given him the authority to investigate conditions in his neighborhood without feeling personally threatened by what he might find.

The SEPTA system might have acted as a legitimizing agency for Kareem, but he couldn't integrate its massive institutional presence with the rest of the world he presented. What he knew about the system was not its politics, its bureaucratic labyrinths, or its relations with the city powerbrokers. He knew the names of the buses and trains and trolleys. He knew SEPTA as a consumer, just as he knew the rest of the economic system as a consumer—and a relatively defenseless consumer at that. SEPTA offered him the power to name routes and connect geographical locations, but the specialized vocabulary he commanded was little more than a list. He couldn't make his knowledge name or control the contradictions that the SEPTA system traverses by track and trolley. Thus the most powerful institution Kareem knew intimately could only reinforce his muteness on issues that impinged on his life.

The best Kareem could do, in my understanding of him, was to name what he could control as a "private" citizen, so to speak, and avoid everything else with vague references and fragmented prose. This kept him out of trouble, but it limited what he could investigate and what world he could conjure in writing. As a single and vulnerable self, he used "bad" writing as his best defense against readers who might want to know about a reality he didn't want to engage. Writing well may be, as Susan Sontag said, the best revenge, but writing poorly has distinct defensive advantages.

On his third rewrite, however, Kareem adopted a different position as an author. He associated himself with the neighborhood that had defeated a crime wave, and suddenly he was no longer a lone self describing a world where he had no power. He was representing the same neighborhood, bringing into prose many of the same community issues, but now he was speaking as a member of a group that had been effective within this world. His writing got "better" because he identified with the neighborhood world where he could say "we" and mean it.

He uses "we" in two senses. In one sense, he associates himself with others who have already claimed for themselves a place as a community. In another sense, however, by writing of a "we," he invents for himself a group to which he can belong. It is one thing to apply for membership in a club, but it is an altogether more significant step to feel yourself a constitutive member of the club by writing its history. An author cannot represent reality in any detail if he has no group sense of identity to back up his claims for what he sees. If there is no adequate sponsoring institution, he must invent one or reconstitute one he had not thought could be his. The achievement of Kareem's third draft is that he takes on the authority of his neighborhood, having himself constituted it as the sponsoring institution for his writing. This is the act of an author.

I said that as a reader I was disconcerted by the course of development in Kareem's drafts. In one respect, Kareem's image of his neighborhood seems overly idealized. He adopts a mythology that the neighborhood can permanently overcome evil, that since they started a "strong town watch" the neighborhood has been "almost totally peaceful." In this formulation he now recognizes strength within the community, where before Kareem looked for it only within himself. This enables him to develop a point of view and an argument, to draw together disparate observations into a coherent essay. But we know that no human grouping can permanently overcome evil, nor is the mythology of even the most admirable groups a complete account of how that group gets and maintains power, distributes rewards, evolves into new stages. The mythology he adopts, however, does not bother me very much. We need a certain amount of enabling fiction to continue staring out into the world, and to write about it for others. I think what bothers me is my own nostalgia for a true individualism.

There is something so appealing to me about the first essays Kareem wrote. I wish I could tear back the page in those essays and find the profound insights Kareem could offer us as an individual unattached to institutional power, with his need to tell a coherent story about himself and his friends. In an all too real way, my sadness at his development is a nostalgia for the idea of the individualistic insight, of the self that pierces to the heart of the ideological beast. I would like to offer my readers the fresh and disturbing observations of Kareem, who looks from below at a society that cares little about him. But this is my delusion, for the possibility of witnessing as an innocent from outside institutional frameworks is no more open to Kareem than it is to me.

The cold and honest fact is that Kareem cannot articulate his position in middle-class society until, at least to some extent, he identifies with that society. As an author, his authority may grow to be more powerful and subtle, allowing him to explore and question the society around him in ways that could very well challenge all its basic assumptions. But I cannot tear away the page that hides his insights, for his insights are exactly what he has written—that the world is a frightening and inhospitable place if you do not feel yourself to be a contributing member to the society that surrounds you and shapes your world.

This nostalgia is perhaps a form of racism, a form easy to find in white teachers working to help dispossessed students from many backgrounds. I am perhaps looking for Kareem and others to do what I never did, and never could do—to leap over the boundaries of institutional authority directly to a commanding position of insight and resistance unmediated by the history of captivity and state control. But to do so would be to entertain what Ralph Ellison warns against in *Invisible Man:* To believe that one can step outside of history in response to the injustices one experiences within it is folly.

The economic metaphor I claimed to find in Kareem's remark about waiting for "tomorrows pay" fits here. The problem with writing for Kareem was that he was not writing for a social structure with which he could truly identify. When I met him, he did not particularly accept the attitude toward schoolwork and books that teachers and successful students share. He wanted to put in his time and leave that world behind when the school bell rang. Yet he wanted what the institutional system had to offer. Only a leap into a frightening and unknown world could give him the power to speak to others, yet it was not a world that seemed to want him.

In the first few months of 1989, my class considered Frederick Douglass's account of his life as a slave. Kareem was the only member of the class who could not see the relevance of Douglass's book to his own life, and he seldom participated in discussions or completed written responses to issues raised by the book. Yet I could not help but feel that Douglass's impassioned plea for education as a means of liberation was written almost expressly for Kareem. It was as if Kareem was caught in the mentality that Douglass associated with the slaves who would not read or plot to escape.

Kareem's struggle with authority reminds me, also, of an experience of another student from Neighborhood Academy. This student graduated from the school some years before Kareem arrived. The student, let me call him Robert, received a scholarship to attend a liberal arts college in western Pennsylvania. Robert went out there during the fall semester, and at Christmastime he returned to see his family. On the way to the store one afternoon during that break, he happened to run into an old girlfriend who lived in the neighborhood. She was irate and began screaming at him. Who did he think he was leaving the neighborhood and never calling or writing her? Did he think he was too good for everyone back home? Suddenly she rushed toward him as if to slap his face, but he felt a sharp pain as she slapped him, and when he touched his cheek he realized that she had been holding a razor blade between her fingers. She had slashed Robert across the face and missed his eye only by fractions of an inch.

That is a story about both Robert and the young woman who had stayed behind. I do not know what happened to the woman, but Robert left college a semester later—a move I would not blame on the woman. There is a leap into the life of dominant institutions that one must take to write "well," to succeed in college, to make one's way in the middle-class world. One leaves behind powerful institutions at home to do that. The violence of the leap, and the fear of leaping, should never be forgotten by those of us who help students along the way. The life waiting for the one who leaps is not nearly as safe and comforting as teachers would like to think, and many, many times kids will choose the dangers of the streets they know to the looming, unknown dangers of failure, rejection, and humiliation that they see ahead of them. Kareem may accomplish the shift, begin to identify with other institutions and come to his own terms with their power, but in the writings and interview he left me an impressive record of just how hard the shift can be.

In sum, Kareem presents one of the great puzzles teachers in city schools often face. Here was a bright, ambitious young man, not on drugs or involved with anything more illegal than sneaking into the movies. He did not even come from the kind of poverty that other kids in the school knew. Yet he often refused, consciously or unconsciously, to engage in schoolwork or the institutional life of a student. I do not offer an answer, a revolutionary new teaching method, or even a resolved analysis of Kareem and his writing. The problems Kareem faced, and urban schooling faces, are too large for simple answers. If I got anywhere with Kareem—and I don't suppose I'll know for years, if at all, whether or not I helped him—it was only by a dogged and firm love. I would not praise him for shoddy work, but I persistently threw back at him a vision of his possibilities. I tried to read his writing seriously, no matter how lightly he took it himself.

The themes that emerge from Kareem's words are undoubtedly the result of patterns within Kareem's own psyche, but they are also themes I have seen again and again in other kids from various Philadelphia neighborhoods. I would not claim Kareem is a type, but I suspect other urban teachers will recognize the picture of Kareem I have presented. Perhaps even more, other teachers may recognize themselves in the account of my efforts to read Kareem's texts and learn what he needs to become an author. My hope for this chapter, indeed for the whole book, is that it will reinforce our collective efforts not to give up on students who produce the sometimes puzzling, half-articulated texts we often encounter in high school and college classrooms.

In many kinds of schools, the questions teachers ask, and the ideas we introduce, are deeply embedded in an institutional world quite different from the one occupied by our students, and thus their answers seem sketchy, disorganized, unconsidered, unduly preoccupied by apparently trivial concerns. With any high school student, we are sometimes apt to ascribe underdeveloped writing to the gap between the adolescent world and the world of adults. We judge too quickly that they are simply not mature enough to write with insight. I don't find that explanation convincing for any student, but for students from marginalized backgrounds the issue is far more grave. They are removed by age, class, and, often, racial barriers from the power centers that drive the middle-class world. Their struggle to gain authority must matter to us.

5

....

Double-Consciousness and Authority

It is a peculiar sensation, this double-consciousness, this sense of always looking at one's self through the eyes of others, of measuring one's soul by the tape of a world that looks on in amused contempt and pity. One ever feels his twoness—an American, a Negro; two souls, two thoughts, two unreconciled strivings; two warring ideals in one dark body, whose dogged strength alone keeps it from being torn asunder.

The history of the American Negro is the history of this strife—this longing to attain self-conscious manhood, to merge his double self into a better and truer self. In this merging he wishes neither of the older selves to be lost. He would not Africanize America, for America has too much to teach the world and Africa. He would not bleach his Negro soul in a flood of white Americanism, for he knows that Negro blood has a message for the world. He simply wishes to make it possible for a man to be both a Negro and an American, without being cursed and spit upon by his fellows, without having the doors of Opportunity closed roughly in his face.

—W.E.B. Du Bois, *The Souls of Black Folk* (3)

Although the above passage has been quoted many times, I have placed it at the head of my concluding chapter because it remains one of the most astute observations about marginalized people in America. Du Bois's contention that "the problem of the Twentieth Century is the problem of the color line" (xxvii) was a prescient recognition that racism would lead to general carnage, from the Holocaust to Apartheid. Even at the turn of the century, the people of the world were pressed against one another to such an extent that Du Bois saw the fate of the whole was dependent on cooperation rather than domination. His vision of a just and effective education is one that embraces the difference between races and traditions and, at the same time, honors the desire in every person to take part in the society we share. Despite the male pronouns, this passage could quite easily apply to the gender line we have come to recognize through feminist critiques. Despite specific references to African-American experience, the dynamics he describes fit Jewish, Hispanic, Asian, or Native American histories within the United States as well. The phenomenon of "double-consciousness" is the manifestation of difference in a society that has desperately sought to deny that difference could matter, or even exist.

All of us have what may be called a private and a public self. The private self is shaped by the institutions associated with our home lives, our neighborhoods, our ethnic traditions. The public self is a result of the interaction between that private self and the larger world of work and economic reward, a world where values drive institutions that affect everyone in the culture. Marginalized people are by definition those whose private selves are at odds with the dominant view of a proper public persona. Du Bois asserts that certain persons feel they must blot out their private selves in order to gain some modicum of public acceptance, even though the culture never seems to accept marginalized people fully, no matter how they cauterize their identities.

From the view of a compositionist and a writer, I would add that a gap between private and public self creates an inhospitable climate for writing. What I find so fascinating about authority as a quality in writing is that, since it is ultimately derived from institutional sponsorship rather than individual stature, a focus on authority helps us to see at least some classic writing problems not as an indication of personal ignorance of "grammar rules" but as a function of social relations between author and sponsor. Writers who are alienated from or insecure within the institutional framework of their writing task will predictably have trouble composing texts for that institution, whether it is a school or a business or a law firm. In my own writing and the writing of my students, no matter what their backgrounds, I see that fragmented and awkward sentences, vague paragraphs, even writer's block often come from the sort of public/private tensions Du Bois terms "double-consciousness."

The stories presented in this book seem to me to offer a picture of authors navigating difference. Writing, and talk about writing, forced Kareem, Maria, and Tita to encounter their own lives as different from other people's, and they each saw the potential for being judged inferior or unacceptable for their difference. They derive their authority from institutions which also define their difference from the dominant culture, and fortunately Neighborhood Academy was nurturing enough that they could explore their home institutions within that school context. They could represent a reality that, they were all aware, might be rejected in disgust or incomprehension by the larger society around them. In this chapter, I consider each student in turn as an author and note what their writing situation may suggest about approaches to other student writers. I conclude with some thoughts about what teachers and researchers can do to alter the nature of double-consciousness for writers struggling to become authors.

First, however, let me return briefly to the theoretical discussion of authority. Earlier, I proposed that we read texts with an awareness of the author's dual role as representative and representer. I said that authors act, through their texts, as agents of the institutions with which they identify themselves (by affiliation, training, accreditation) and at the same time they represent, realize, or bring to life realities sponsored by those institutions. Thus the power of an authority is in large part dependent upon the social standing of the institution or institutions from which a writer derives his or her status as an author. For example, a *Scientific American* article on supernovas, coauthored by two astronomers employed in prestigious research centers, would offer a fairly unproblematic performance of authority. The journals and papers of Kareem, Maria, and Tita show us a sort of authority in written texts that is far more complex and pitted with the gaps between cultures, classes, and races in American society.

The work of M. M. Bakhtin adds a valuable gloss on the stories I have presented and Du Bois's observations about double-consciousness. Like Du Bois, Bakhtin sees the individual poised between a private world and a public one. Like Du Bois, he recognizes this position as one fraught with danger and struggle. Bakhtin adds to this picture the almost palpable presence of language itself as the medium and meetingplace for clashing worlds. Bakhtin can serve as a bridge between Du Bois's political and social observations and the pedagogical, linguistic, and cognitive concerns of writing instructors and researchers.

As Michael Holquist has noted, Bakhtin uses various formulations, in various texts, to explore a "master opposition," which Holquist identifies as "the conflict between a set of values grounded in the self, and a set of values grounded in the other" ("Politics of Representation" 179). Bakhtin's opposition is between "heteroglossia" and "canonization" (see, for example, "Discourse in the Novel" 270ff). *Heteroglossia* is the tendency in language toward stratification, diversity, and randomness, and the Russian critic associates it with the "behavioral" ideology of the self in formation. It is language as people live within it, telling their stories day to day in the evolving talk of personal, family, and neighborhood concerns. Canonization, on the other hand, is Bakhtin's name for the tendency in language toward unification, stability, and authority, and he associates it with the shared values of an "official" or public ideology. Here language gets purified, specialized, standardized by those who use words with the power of a society behind them. Holquist argues that Bakhtin uses this same logic to revise Freud's famous distinction between conscious and unconscious realities. Bakhtin sees both as conscious, but the former is "official" while the latter is "unofficial" and thus subject to the mechanism of censorship ("Politics of Representation" 177).

Bakhtin's discussion of this opposition in "Discourse in the Novel" (*Dialogic Imagination* 259–422) is particularly suited to a conception of authority as informed by social context. Bakhtin asserts that an opposition of discourses informs "an individual's ideological becoming, in the most fundamental sense" (342). In Bakhtin's view, any speaker's consciousness is shaped by the "dialogic interrelationship" between "authoritative discourse" and "internally persuasive discourse." He describes

> a sharp gap between these two categories: in one, the authoritative word (religious, political, moral; the word of a father, of adults and of teachers, etc.) that does not know internal persuasiveness, in the other internally persuasive word that is denied all privilege, backed up by no authority at all, and is frequently not even acknowledged in society (not by public opinion, nor by scholarly norms, nor by criticism), not even in the legal code. (342)

Thus, these two categories of discourse are distinguished by their relative distance from powerful social institutions. One is linked to everything in society that defines right and wrong while the other is characterized by its lack of support from those sponsoring institutions.

The situation of double-consciousness that Du Bois describes—and that I believe Kareem, Maria, and Tita face—adds yet another coil to the complex windings in Bakhtin's account of dialogical communication. It would be easy, but profoundly wrong, to associate the world of nonstandard urban vernacular speech with the "unofficial" or unsanctioned discourse of Bakhtin's behavioral ideology. To do so would be to fall into the trap of seeing subjugated cultures as "primitive" and thus more childlike or wilder than dominant cultures. On the contrary, urban high school students, like all writers, face more than one form of authoritative discourse. In their home worlds, kids in marginalized communities must negotiate the languages of power associated with churches, family relationships, public services, and organized crime. At the same time, like all students, they must also come to terms with the authoritative discourse of teachers and school books. What makes double-consciousness so treacherous is that, where middle-class children learn a discourse at home and in the neighborhood that is compatible with the power relations at school, working-class or aid-dependent children must accommodate themselves to multiple authoritative discourses, each of which may oppose one another in certain essential ways.

Tita, for instance, struggles in her journal with the language of authority spoken on the street as well as with the very different but equally powerful authority of her father's church. Yet when she faces the authority of college discourse, she must struggle on yet another front to maintain a positive allegiance to home institutions that the college world tends to treat as a barely perceptible and undifferentiated subculture. Middle-class children may also face differing authoritative languages, but the voices of authority in their lives tend to harmonize into a unified set of power relationships. In a suburban neighborhood, the baseball coach, the minister, and parents may differ over values and priorities, but they will not be at odds for long. If they do clash, Dad and Mom will take Sis off the team or out of Sunday school—or they will come to an understanding with the other authorities.

In neighborhoods where financial and political power is scarce, a child hears voices in a deafening discord. One cannot follow Mama's advice one day and then watch her be humiliated at the welfare office the next without registering the conflict between home and public institutions. Every North Philadelphia kid knows about dealers who humbly troop off to jail one day and triumphantly return to their corners the next. And, perhaps most tellingly, no African-American or Latino parent (of any economic class or political persuasion) can teach his or her children that the policeman is always and forever their friend.

Having rejected the notion that students like Maria, Tita, and Kareem do not participate in "official" discourse, I would still agree that the dominant culture may regard even the most "official" language that Neighborhood Academy students speak as nonauthoritative and insubstantial. Maria's situation suggests an instructive hypothetical example. Since high school romances are cute and inconsequential in the middle-class culture that puts off serious adult relationships until after college, the depth and reality of Maria's relationship with her boyfriend's mother cannot be valued as an integral part of Maria's sense of herself as someone with something to say. The well-meaning college composition teacher who assigns an essay on "an important personal relationship" will probably only get a truncated and muted account of Maria's bond with Felix's mom, for the institution that gives that relationship power and substance has no palpable existence within a college classroom. Maria's relationship with Delores is "personal," but it is also deeply rooted in social institutions that most white, middle-class teachers would not recognize, especially within the bland, cinderblock classroom environment where the personal is seen as the "starting point" on the road to grand decontextualized ideas. Given even Maria's best effort to comply with the assignment, what the teacher receives and reads will likely appear coded, involuted, enigmatic. The assignment will seem to have failed, and so will Maria. No single person is evil or lazy in that hypothetical writing situation; the institutional environment itself can wither the most promising projects.

But we could alter in significant ways that hypothetical personal essay assignment Maria might receive from her college composition teacher. Rather than use that essay as a warm-up to other, more academic assignments, the composition teacher might use the essay as the basis for a large-scale introduction to intellectual investigation. After Maria and her class had written their first renderings of relationships as personal, they could read essays on family structure, on psychodynamics, on male and female roles, and write another rendering of their relationship using some techniques they had learned from a close analysis of those readings. Then they could read a novel or a few short stories that centered on intimate relationships and could try their hands at "fictionalizing" what they had just dissected. Perhaps they could conclude this unit of a composition course by writing a meditation on what they had learned in the process of seeing the same relationship through a series of interpretive frameworks.

My point here is not to propose a model composition course. Approaches such as Bartholomae and Petrosky's composition course centered on adolescence (*Facts*), or Kiniry and Rose's wide-ranging textbook on "critical strategies in academic discourse" demonstrate that composition can be taught with an eye to institutional setting and the self in a sea of public discourse. If we begin to see a writer's authority in a social context, then we can avoid making the common mistakes that come from operating composition instruction (especially in "remedial" programs) as a technological training course designed to "equip" students with "skills." A skills theory of composition only heightens the pain of double-consciousness by seeking to ignore the dilemma, suggesting somehow that if you can learn to brandish the comma superbly then cultural conflict will melt away.

This is not to say that skills have no value, as long as we see them as habits specific to an institution rather than as badges of absolute intelligence or worth. I will argue later in this chapter that there is a very real reason for making school codes and expectations explicit. Outsiders need good maps to navigate inner institutional channels successfully. But there is more to writing instruction than "outside" and "inside" (see Lyon, "Interdisciplinarity," for a critique of the territory metaphor). Du Bois's challenge to us is to find a way to open doors while still respecting the nature of the person who passes the threshold.

Kareem, Maria, and Tita each in their own way contribute to the picture I have assembled of institutionally derived authority. In my account of their writing and social context, sometimes story takes precedent over analysis because I am convinced that we cannot understand authority either as a catalogued feature of the text or a diagnosable factor within the psyche of the writer. I wish to comment on the sort of authors I imagine each of these student-writers to be. But I must warn that my "conclusions" about the three Neighborhood Academy students are merely my last narrative intrusion into the collective story, more like stage directions for the final scene of a collaboratively written drama than the assured argument of a scientist summing up results of a five-year study.

Kareem responded with silence against the "personalness" of writing. Yet when he identified with a community, he did author a revealing and extensive account of his world. The prose of the first two drafts of his neighborhood paper is awkward and unhelpful to the reader, but his "poor" writing serves the purpose of preventing the reality Kareem represents from appearing too problematic and unmanageable. He seems to be so aware that his home self might be attacked, rejected, or denied significance that he prefers proud inarticulateness to painful revelation. I have suggested that his writing offers a paradox frustrating for a teacher. I see Kareem as a vulnerable person who shows a tough exterior, and his very toughness prevents him from drawing on his real strengths. He controls the material objects of his world with lists and description and simultaneously gives up the rewards that deeper explorations of patterns and causes might bring him. Kareem can't take up those deeper explorations on his own, for they require manipulating the vocabulary of established domains like history, economics, sociology, literature, all of which he seems to regard with distrust. The bind of having to maintain a tight-lipped public persona to protect a vulnerable private self makes writing a stressful and dangerous labor for him. This is the bind of double-consciousness.

The third draft of Kareem's neighborhood paper suggests the power of institutional sponsorship. Once he felt he was writing for something larger and more defensible than himself, he could afford to consider a serious problem in his world, and in the process he could present a more coherent and sustained narration. Even writing about the public transportation system could not give him the backing that his neighborhood did for a prose that explores a complicated issue. The writing could get "better" because he had a stake in representing in written language the reality of the neighborhood fight against crime. In Du Bois's terms, the third draft provided an opportunity for Kareem to integrate his "Negro" self, the life he lives and witnesses at home, with his "American" self, the one that can be presented in school and in standard written English. As I have said, a crucial issue of authority is the extent to which the author feels identified with the institution or institutions sponsoring the writing. A corollary of this assertion would be that the idea of the institution must be developed enough in the writer's mind and in his world to provide an adequate sense of shelter and viability for him to speak as an author in its service. Kareem embraced the entities of Mount Airy and of school life at Neighborhood Academy enough to produce the text of his third draft.

This brings up a vital point about the function of school as a sponsoring institution for writers who do not come from classes and communities that traditionally send kids to college. A school can never be, in 1960s parlance, truly "free." That is to say, even the most neighborhood-friendly school has an institutional life of its own that influences the job student-writers do as authors. My concern is that schools should serve to support students about who they already are as thinkers and members of a family and neighborhood network and allow students to grow as their thinking becomes more bold and searching. We should help students find *projects* they can care about and offer advice, criticism, even evaluation in the spirit of enabling that project to prosper. In this way, the school comes to cosponsor writing that draws its institutional authority from other sources which the student finds necessary or congenial.

The double-consciousness that Du Bois describes is especially destructive if the public persona an author is called upon to develop is made impossible by distance from sponsoring institutions. If you cannot imagine yourself as an anthropologist, you cannot write anthropology. If you cannot imagine yourself a poet, you cannot write a poem. If you cannot imagine your neighborhood as a collective entity, you cannot write using a community "we." On the other hand, if a writer develops an identification with an institution that can sponsor his or her writing, then that sort of writing becomes possible. It seems reasonable to think that most writers, especially minority or low-income students, are more likely to develop their first fruitful identifications with the home institutions they know best. This means something more than assignments in basic writing classes centering upon home topics such as church functions, high school graduation, family outings. It means that authorityless writers are more likely to feel themselves authors—to feel what it is like to have something to say to an audience— if they are called upon to represent home institutions rather than the school-related institutions they may find alien.

I think, for instance, of the two students from the University of Wisconsin whom I mentioned briefly in chapter 2. Both were African-American women from poor neighborhoods in large cities. Both had been identified before freshmen year as basic writers, but both worked very hard to do well in courses that required papers. One decided to go into nursing, the other into education. Each wrote a paper in her sophomore year that functioned as a turning point for her as a writer. The nursing student wrote a long paper about health problems in the black community for a class on contemporary health issues. The education major wrote a paper called "Black Female Education: A National and Personal History" for a history class. In that paper she combined an historical overview of the schooling of African-American women with a personal account of her experience in school contrasted with accounts from her mother and grandmother. These papers gave their authors the opportunity to speak as representatives of their own communities in the university while they could also act as representatives of their chosen professions to their home communities. In such writing situations, students managed—for the moment—to bring their "two-ness" into a unity that obliterated neither "older self."

Maria was more secure than Kareem in writing about her social world and, given encouragement from her readers, could explore that world in both journal writing and formal expository prose. Yet she was deathly afraid that people outside her neighborhood would talk about her behind her back, would criticize her for being different. In my class, when she wrote about subjects outside her social sphere, her writing seemed vaguer, less directed—she lost her authority. This did not stop me from giving her assignments to write about Nathaniel Hawthorne characters or scenes from Frederick Douglass's autobiography, and I do not think teachers should hesitate to ask any writing student to take on issues outside their home experience. However, I do think it is important that students like Maria get ample opportunity to return again and again to the themes and challenges made most real by the frame of social institutions they know from long experience. The strength of her writing "self" derived from a consciousness of the many voices that constituted the reality of her neighborhood, and her sense of the power of language derived from the way words work among the people she knew. In college, it may take her a long time to know intimately people who have power in the middle class world; only if Maria can find a way to preserve some of the authority she carries with her from the neighborhood will she thrive as a writer in college.

Tita's personal writing is almost heroic in the way it continues to explore and represent her reality despite the pain in her home life. Of the three students I discuss in this study, she was the most identified with school as an institution. Her story reminds us that some students from marginalized backgrounds will not necessarily feel empowered by representing home institutions like family and church, and teachers should not automatically think that one approach will fit all students, even those from the same neighborhood (see Rodriguez, *Hunger of Memory,* for a very different version of the public and private language clash). This was what I found so valuable about the friendship between Tita and Maria: they each had different sources of strength, Maria at home and Tita at school, and they found a way to pool their strength and to help each other along. Their friendship points out that all the ingenious individual assignments in the world cannot inculcate what a supportive comradeship can teach.

Synthia Fordham has written convincingly about the "racelessness" she found in African-American students—especially young women— who were successful in the city high school she studied. She sees in a group of students who make good grades a tendency to reject cultural ways their peers identify as "black," perhaps in the hope of further assimilating into white America (58). However, I do not think it is entirely fair to accuse those students of denying their racial origins in order to get ahead. The situation for those who want to achieve in the dominant culture is as complex as it is demanding. The dominant culture still does not recognize marks of racial or ethnic origin as positive traits, and double-consciousness can still be as painful as it was in Du Bois's day. At the same time, as Fordham points out, successful minority students are often shunned by their peers (80). We should not ennoble home life to such an extent that we blind ourselves to the damage that some of its institutions can cause children. It is not surprising that some students would want to leave the trappings of home life behind, even if later on they learn how to embrace home institutions that do offer them continued support. This dynamic of flight and return certainly occurs in middle-class families. Why shouldn't it also obtain under other economic conditions?

Tita testified to her fierce devotion to Puerto Rican culture. Still,

her strong commitment to education and "getting ahead" compelled
her to try what she feared she could not do. Like many Neighborhood
Academy students, Tita surely had times when the hours she spent in
school were some of the most peaceful and secure hours of her day. It
was necessary for her to identify with school culture rather than the
more heinous elements of street life. The interview she did with the
two brothers—one a drug dealer and dropout, the other a school success—was emblematic of her own need to develop a certain academic
distance from the street yet represent its reality. As teachers, we want
to protect students from unnecessary pain when we can, but we also
must let students grapple with difficult questions of identity and social
standing, hoping that they will come to a balance that includes the best
of many institutional worlds.

This brings me to concluding remarks about pedagogy and theory,
with the focus not on students but on teachers and researchers. I want
to consider how we can use our power in the classroom and the academic world to make authority in written language a little less myste-
rious, less shrouded in ritual and unexpressed regulation. I want to look
at the argument Lisa Delpit makes in "The Silenced Dialogue," for I
believe she offers an insight into how we might address the problem of
double-consciousness in basic writers, and how we might bridge the
gulf between the institutions that sponsor writing in their home settings
and in the academy. Delpit, above all, has much to say about our own
position as "gatekeepers" to the institutional life of the dominant culture.

In her discussion of the silenced dialogue between white and nonwhite educators, Delpit argues that her liberal colleagues least like saying aloud what we most need to name: that language and language
instruction is associated with power, and that teachers serve a very real
gatekeeping function for society whether they wish to acknowledge that
function or not. She outlines a "culture of power" ("Silenced Dialogue" 282) that exists in even the most progressive classrooms and
warns us that to pretend that students need not learn about the codes
in the culture of power is to do a pronounced disservice to students
from marginalized groups:

> I further believe that to act as if power does not exist is to ensure
> that the power status quo remains the same. To imply to children

or adults (but of course the adults won't believe you anyway) that it doesn't matter how you talk or how you write is to ensure their ultimate failure. I prefer to be honest with my students. Tell them that their language and cultural style is unique and wonderful but that there is a political power game that is also being played, and if they want to be in on that game there are certain games that they too must play. ("Silenced Dialogue" 292)

By using the metaphor of "the game," Delpit does not intend to dismiss all education as mere finishing for polite society. She is concerned that students learn to make meaning and develop intellectually, goals that she by no means regards cynically. By the end of "The Silenced Dialogue," she asserts that the debate between "skills" and "process" writing instruction—the issue she focused on in her earlier article, "Skills and Other Dilemmas of a Progressive Black Educator"—is "fallacious," and that both approaches are necessary not only to address "the need to help students to establish their own voices" but also "to coach those voices to produce notes that will be heard clearly in the larger society" ("Silenced Dialogue" 296). But she is acutely aware of the ease with which the dominant culture can look through children and adults who do not express themselves in standard English and show facility with conventional forms. In both articles, she presents the testimony of nonwhite teachers about their frustration with labels of "traditionalist" and "authoritarian" because their classrooms are more teacher-centered and skills-oriented than their white colleagues' classrooms. Like them, she recognizes that there is a "game" with terribly high stakes that children must learn to play in school and beyond.

It is not my purpose here to recapitulate Delpit's argument, nor to evaluate her position and the recent responses to it. I do think reactions, such as Herbert Kohl's rather negative response to Delpit in *The Nation*, center far too much on Delpit's article "Skills and Other Dilemmas" and therefore miss the wider import of her analysis of the relationship between the white educational establishment and nonwhite students and educators. I would like to apply her recognition of the need to make codes explicit to an exchange I had with Kareem and noted in chapter 4. Mistakes are often more enlightening than exemplary performances, and the disjunction this exchange reveals is more eloquent than calls I can make for teachers to pay attention to code interpretation in writing classrooms. I see no point in remaining silently ashamed of my mistakes; I can't help Kareem any more now, but, if a discussion of one mistake helps others to understand the nature of the problem, at least I might manage to squeeze some redeeming value from my obtuseness.

During the April interview with Kareem, we touched on an incident that had happened in class just a day or two before. I asked him if the assignments relating to Frederick Douglass's autobiography were too "personal," and Kareem responded: "No, but I told you I didn't know how you wanted me to do it, but when we got to class and Danny started it off and I was like oh is that what he wanted us to do, just tell what's going on, that's—I knew I could do that."

This remark should have been a tip-off to me, but I was unable to hear what amounted to a call for help. I think he really was a bit mystified by much of what I had been asking him to do all semester. That late in the year I was not as focused on summarizing, how to "just tell what's going on," in favor of more sophisticated analyses of texts. But clearly he was not comfortable with summary as a process. The "skill" of summarizing involves much more than decoding words, but it is not limited to the rhetorical issues of how sentences build one on another in a passage. The school behavior of "telling what's going on" is also an extremely reassuring one for students who are not on their home turf in school. During language acquisition, a toddler looking out her apartment window may exclaim "Plane!," and her father may say approvingly "Yes, airplane." This is a vital moment for her growing sense that the language she is using is anchored in both her and her parents' experiences. In the same way, Kareem and Danny may well have needed much more assurance that what they saw in a text was also what I saw, and that we could share the unfolding drama of "what's going on" before we could talk at length about why the drama might be going on.

I probably couldn't hear Kareem when he made the above remark in our interview because I was angry that he had been "withdrawn" all semester. Quite honestly, I thought he had been lazy, unwilling to put the work into the course that others had managed. I will not entirely rule out laziness because I do not want to relieve Kareem of responsibility for his own school performance. It would be easy for me to blame myself entirely for his lackluster schoolwork, but that would show too little respect for him and his possibilities. It is, however, also possible that I just did not put together the right mixture of assignments in summary, conclusion drawing, and speculation to give him a strong enough grounding in the cultural norms of a collegelike classroom. In any case, I responded to him in the interview with a rebuke whose gentleness (from my point of view) only makes the underlying message that much more mystical and discouraging:

> Well, for instance, you missed what Maria did the other day, and what she did is probably a little closer to what I originally assigned—I mean, I don't mind what you guys were doing today, but—what we were getting at was what were the main ideas underneath it, whereas what you guys were doing was saying what was going on step by step.

It is true that Kareem had missed class the day Maria gave what I thought was a model presentation, and his absences always frustrated me. But it is also true that Danny and Kareem had enacted, in class, a model of reading they were willing and even eager to produce. In a sense, I wasn't paying close enough attention to them. To serve them better as a teacher, I probably should have built a series of assignments that highlighted the process of summarizing "what was going on step by step" and not been so eager to go on to discover "the main ideas underneath." I still believe that "higher" and "lower" critical skills should be taught together rather than in separate, discrete stages, but I may have asked Kareem and Danny to engage too quickly and too completely in a kind of discourse whose rules they may not adequately have understood. I'm sure I could have been more explicit about the kind of answers expected in seminar-type settings.

I do not mean to bring my discussion around to Piaget-like cognitive stages. Instead, I'm suggesting that summarizing and drawing conclusions are games we play in school, games whose rules and procedures are not often made fully explicit to students. Earlier in the year, I had worked on summarizing passages in Hawthorne and Poe, but I assumed that Douglass's text was "straightforward" enough to allow us to move on to "higher order" thinking about it. I think now that I didn't work enough on the skill of reading a passage as one is expected to read it in college. Granted, college teachers complain about the lack of such skills in most of their students. However, I feel that I could have had a greater effect on the school performance of Kareem and others if I had been a little less anxious to hold great discussions and a little more patient in teaching the procedure of accepted classroom discussion. I would still not give up the sparkle and excitement of our best class sessions; students need to get excited about ideas even if they don't fully understand them. I only wish I had taught them to account for their reading more consistently and rigorously because I know that is what their teachers will want from them in the future.

Delpit also points out that it is not only the student who must be taught explicitly about codes: the teacher must also learn to be constantly aware of the culture of power that surrounds and informs pedagogical practice (see Bartholomae, "Inventing the University," and Bizzell, "Power, Authority"). My experiences at Neighborhood Academy and elsewhere lead me to agree enthusiastically with Delpit's observation that "those with power are frequently least aware of—or at least willing to acknowledge—its existence. Those with less power are often most aware of its existence" ("Silenced Dialogue" 283). I am willing to say that the majority of my mistakes as a teacher have been a result of forgetting how much power I have over what students accept as true, correct, and "normal" in my own classroom. I have sometimes left assignments, projects, and discussions so open that students felt intimidated rather than encouraged, vulnerable rather than safe.

I have been most successful when I have exercised my power to set up clear boundaries and limits within which students could strive in new ways and feel responsible for what they produced. The best situation is not for teachers to abdicate power, but just the reverse. Following Delpit's logic, an "abdication" of power on the part of the teacher is merely a way of upholding the power arrangement teachers do not acknowledge. The best situation is when teachers exercise power so that they enable students to exercise their own power. This sort of responsible use of power is at the heart of any school-home institutional cooperation.

After a talk I gave at a conference on material from chapter 4, a person in the audience said to me: "You talk about the neighborhood as the sponsoring institution for Kareem's third draft, but isn't the sponsoring institution still the school?" I answered something about the complex of sponsors in writing, but I didn't feel very satisfied with my answer. Later on that evening, I met my questioner, whose name was Art. We tried together to understand the arrangement. For me, Delpit's insistence that the school or the teacher can never resign its power makes the question a crucial one. Finally, I had to give Art an analogy as a provisional answer. School functions like the sun in relation to other stars in the sky. It shines so brightly that other lights seem not to illuminate anything, and only when the sun is set or eclipsed can other lights show their brilliance. The trick would be to shade out the sun, eclipse it, or work in the dark so that other lights can have their day.

But my analogy lends too much "naturalness" to the power of schools. A school is not a celestial body like the sun, though it does have a similar predictability and unconscious public effect. It does have an insistent presence—and a power it cannot resign—but it can be an active partner with its students rather than a passive dispenser of knowledge. If we are committed to seeing the world using different light sources, we can learn how to do it. Schools can be restructured and teachers can rewrite curricula. Students can reach outside school walls for research, internships, mentors. It cannot be done, however, without a conscious struggle against the overwhelming naturalness of the school's institutional inertia. Only when we work hard to foster other forms of sponsorship can they thrive in the daylight of school experience.

I still haven't answered Art to my own satisfaction. Part of Delpit's point is that students *will* live in a school environment, and it is cruel to pretend they won't need to learn the ways of school skills. Teaching the five-paragraph theme—that dreaded artifact of current-traditional methodology—is a good example of what Delpit means by making codes explicit. I am strongly against teaching the five-paragraph theme as an absolute, a position I suspect Delpit would share. However, I make a point to teach it as one form to every class of students who have been identified as "basic" writers. I teach it with humor and a little irony, as though it were a private joke I am letting students in on, but I teach the rigors of its seemingly simple conventions nonetheless. It *is* a private joke, and some writers are not privy to the information they need to laugh at it. The five-paragraph theme is far more than a dull little exercise requiring an introduction, three body paragraphs, and a conclusion, all in the service of a tidy thesis. Its demand for a "main point," its peculiar type of linear argumentation, its decontextualized and depersonalized sense of "evidence" or "proof" is characteristic of what almost all college teachers want in their students papers, no matter what their orientation toward the writing process.

To teach students to write for school, without making them aware of the idea of a paper held in the minds of a hundred thousand college professors, is truly to "create situations in which students ultimately find themselves held accountable for knowing a set of rules about which no one has ever directly informed them" (Delpit, "Silenced Dialogue" 287). Without understanding the very profound social message carried by the five-paragraph theme form, students are extremely vulnerable when they enter the public arena of school. Similarly, white-collar employees are extremely vulnerable if they do not understand the formal demands of the office memo. It does not matter how much authority writers may have as members of their own culture. Without an understanding of the institutional codes and procedures the dominant culture expects to see exhibited in writing, marginalized people cannot "produce the notes that will be heard in the larger society," as Delpit says ("Silenced Dialogue" 296). Unless teachers and researchers make a concerted effort to make middle-class codes explicit, taking up a public persona will remain for our students a painful and vulnerable role to play.

But Art's question remains for me an open challenge to the structure that makes school, or any dominating institution, so difficult to maneuver around. I do not merely want to fit writers like Maria, Tita, and Kareem into the school; the school itself must change to meet new challenges to its responsibility as a sponsoring institution. That, indeed, is what makes school different from other sponsoring institutions. Corporations and governments want authors who will carry out objectives that may have little to do with the well-being of the authors themselves. I would like to change the center of gravity in those institutions also, but I can have more influence in the school setting. Schools supposedly sponsor writing in order to educate the writer. If education can be defined as more open-ended and wide-ranging than job training, then schools have the opportunity to work actively with home institutions that in large part define their students.

A call for schools to cosponsor writing goes beyond either the 1960s cry for "relevance" and the present debate over expanding the canon. Schools cannot share their legitimating power with neighborhoods, local churches, and families unless they are prepared to honor nonacademic experience as real and worthy of notice. We must come to accept as valuable and meaningful the private lives and home institutions that have always been removed from powerful public concerns. It is one thing to make room for Toni Morrison and Leslie Marmon Silko on the American literature syllabus. It is quite another to encourage students to learn how to write history by tracing their family's movements over the last hundred years, or political science by researching a public debate of particular importance in their neighborhoods, or literary criticism by analyzing the stories their grandparents tell. And are we willing to allow students to move *away* from the thesis-driven essay if it means they are learning how to use prose in a more exploratory way in successive drafts?

The painfulness of double-consciousness comes from the untenable position marginalized persons must take. On the one hand, a person like Maria is asked in college to achieve in a foreign environment governed by unspoken rules which in the end may never permit her full citizenship. On the other hand, the same person is asked to accept the definition of her home institutions as peculiar, counterproductive, insignificant—perhaps even the factor holding her back from wholehearted acceptance into the "mainstream." But isn't this an old argument? Didn't the black power movement fight this battle in the 1960s? Yet the battle remains to be fought again, maybe this time over subtle yet more pervasive problems. Apparently, this time the solutions will not come in the form of law and policy changes. During the civil rights movement the need was to overturn Jim Crow laws. Now we must learn to overturn habits of reading and writing which enforce Jim Crow–like lines with the ferocity of attack dogs but which attract no more attention than the barely audible hum of air conditioning in a college library.

I can hear Delpit urging me to prepare kids for classes that have little to do with the places they come from and the people they know. But I don't want to limit students to subjects that they can "relate" to in some narrow sense. In the end, I must go back to the assertion I made at the beginning of this book. Students from neighborhoods or ethnic groups or social classes that are marginalized by the dominant culture are both different from and similar to all other students. They come from homes and streets not usually represented with any kind of fullness or accuracy in the textbooks or the movies. They don't feel terribly welcome in schools—particularly in colleges—that take other children's backgrounds for granted. When they go to college, they don't have the money they imagine (not always correctly) that their white peers do. They also may come from extreme and sometimes violent situations at home that make the hours spent in school some of their safest and calmest times. Thus they need the institution to act responsibly toward them, to include them and to make a nurturing space for them. At the same time, city kids (or kids from Indian reservations or rural farm towns) need what any student in school needs—to be taught by teachers who respect them, who both invite and demand hard work and emotional investment from them. They need to be clear about what their teachers expect of them and what the rules of the game will be.

Compositionists need to focus both on the individual and the institutional setting, on the private and the public self of writers trying to become authors. How many factors and contradictory forces can we include in our picture of authorityless authors? How willing will we be to alter our institutions in order to educate and employ the whole American population, regardless of difference and divisions? No "model" will ever be definitive, nor will any one program provide all the answers to educational problems faced by students at the margins. Provisional solutions must be creative and fair, curricula and programs must never be allowed to lapse into self-contented tradition. Above all, educators must be convinced that every child deserves an equal chance to grow to her or his full stature within a nation that can value a wide range of cultural contributions.

In the area of research, I think we must devote new attention to the way that writers from marginalized groups come to see themselves positioned within colleges, businesses, government agencies. I think we need to know more about what brings a writer to think of herself or himself as an author. To my mind, this will involve compositionists in a welter of stories. We'll have to be prepared to discuss public and private, individual and group, self and society, official and unofficial in terms that are not oppositional or dualistic but dialectic or, indeed, contradictory and multiform. The day of flowcharts is over, but a purely sociological conception cannot satisfy us either. Kareem, Maria, and Tita remain distinct persons to me, and that is an impression I can never forget as a teacher or a student of writing.

I return to the positive vision of Du Bois, to his image of a "better and truer self" that merges public and private personas harmoniously. Authority draws on institutions that shape and are shaped in both public and private spheres, and we can not neglect any part of a writer's social reality in analyzing his or her composing process. I hope that someday the passage from Du Bois with which I began this chapter will appear quaint and dated. To render it so will take a major change in our social and economic order. For the present, composition must, at the very least, attend to the effect cultural conditions have on writers at the margins of power in contemporary society.

Bibliography

The following is a bibliography of books and articles that have in some fairly specific way made this book possible. I include here works I have referred to in the text, but I also include writing by authors I haven't mentioned but who exerted an important influence on my ideas about authority and my way of telling the stories of the Neighborhood Academy students. For example, I do not mention in the text either Shirley Brice Heath's *Ways With Words* nor Sandra Gilbert and Susan Gubar's *Madwoman in the Attic,* and yet these two books were crucial to the ambition and theoretical framework of my project. Of course, my intention here is not merely to list my favorite books in the field—I just want to give an honest account of the authors who helped bring this project to the page. Hopefully, readers new to basic writing pedagogy or urban education will find some useful references here, but this bibliography is by no means an exhaustive list in those fields.

Annas, Pamela. "Style as Politics: A Feminist Approach to the Teaching of Writing." *College English* 47.4 (1985): 360–71.

Applebee, A. N. *Writing in the Secondary School: English and the Content Areas.* Research Report No. 21. Urbana: NCTE, 1981.

Ascher, C. "Helping Hispanic Students to Complete High School and Enter College." *Urban Review* 17.1 (1985): 65–72.

Bakhtin, M. M. *The Dialogic Imagination.* Trans. Caryl Emerson and Michael Holquist. Ed. Michael Holquist. Austin: U of Texas P, 1981.

Bartholomae, David. "Inventing the University." *Perspectives on Literacy.* Ed. Eugene R. Kintgen, Barry M. Kroll, and Mike Rose. Carbondale, IL: S. Illinois UP, 1988. 273–85.

Bartholomae, David, and Anthony Petrosky. *Facts, Artifacts and Counterfacts: Theory and Method for a Reading and Writing Course.* Portsmouth, NH: Boynton/Cook-Heinemann, 1986.

Berger, Peter L., and Thomas Luckmann. *The Social Construction of Reality.* New York: Anchor-Doubleday, 1967.

Bernstein, Basil. "Social Class, Language, and Socialization." *Language and Social Context.* Ed. P. P. Giglioli. Harmondsworth, Eng.: Penguin, 1972.

Berthoff, Ann. *The Making of Meaning.* Upper Montclair, NJ: Boynton/Cook, 1981.

Bizzell, Patricia. *Academic Discourse and Critical Consciousness.* Pittsburgh: U of Pittsburgh P, 1992.

———. "Power, Authority, and Critical Pedagogy." *Journal of Basic Writing* 10.2 (Fall 1991): 54–70.

Bowler, R., et al. "Self-Esteem and Interracial Attitudes in Black High School Students: A Comparison with Five Other Ethnic Groups." *Urban Education* 21 (Apr. 1986): 3–19.

Brandt, Deborah. *Literacy as Involvement: The Acts of Writers, Readers, and Texts.* Carbondale, IL: Southern Illinois UP, 1990.

———. "Toward an Understanding of Context in Composition." *Written Communication* 3.2 (1986): 139–57.

Britton, James, et al. *The Development of Writing Abilities (11–18).* London: Macmillan Education, 1975.

Brodkey, Linda. *Academic Writing as Social Practice.* Philadelphia: Temple UP, 1987.

Brooke, Robert E. "Underlife and Writing Instruction." *College Composition and Communication* 38 (1987): 141–53.

———. *Writing and Sense of Self: Identity Negotiation in Writing Workshops.* Urbana: NCTE, 1991.

Brooks, Charlotte K., ed. *Tapping Potential: English and Language Arts for the Black Learner.* Urbana: NCTE, 1985.

Cleary, Linda M. "A Profile of Carlos: Strengths of a Non-Standard Dialect Writer." *English Journal* 77 (Sept. 1988): 59–64.

Clifford, John, and John Schilb. "Composition Theory and Literary Theory." *Perspectives on Research and Scholarship in Composition.* Ed. Ben W. McClelland and Timothy R. Donovan. New York: MLA, 1985. 45–67.

Cooper, Marilyn M. "The Ecology of Writing." *College English* 48.4 (1986): 364–75.

Cummins, J. "Empowering Minority Students: A Framework for Intervention." *Harvard Educational Review* 56 (Feb. 1986): 18–36.

Delpit, Lisa P. "The Silenced Dialogue: Power and Pedagogy in Educating Other People's Children." *Harvard Educational Review* 58.3 (1988): 280–98.

———. "Skills and Other Dilemmas of a Progressive Black Educator." *Harvard Educational Review* 56.4 (1986): 379–85.

Douglass, Frederick. *Narrative of the Life of Frederick Douglass, an American Slave.* 1845. New York: Signet, 1968.

Du Bois, W. E. Burghardt. *The Souls of Black Folk.* 1903. New York: Washington Square P, 1970.

Dyson, Anne H. "Writing and the Social Lives of Children." *Language Arts* 62 (Oct. 1985): 632–39.

Elbow, Peter. "Closing My Eyes as I Speak: An Argument for Ignoring Audience." *College English* 49.1 (1987): 50–69.

————. "Toward a Phenomenology of Freewriting." *Journal of Basic Writing* 8.2 (Fall 1989): 42–71.

Eliot, T. S. "Tradition and the Individual Talent." *Selected Essays of T. S. Eliot.* 1932. New York: Harcourt Brace Jovanovich, 1964. 3–11.

Ellison, Ralph. *Invisible Man.* 1947. New York: Vintage, 1972.

Emig, Janet. *The Composing Processes of Twelfth Graders.* Research Report No. 13. Urbana: NCTE, 1971.

Faigley, Lester. "Competing Theories of Process: A Critique and a Proposal." *College English* 48.6 (1986): 527–42.

Faigley, Lester, Roger D. Cherry et al. *Assessing Writers' Knowledge and Processes of Composing.* Norwood, NJ: Ablex, 1985.

Fairbanks, Colleen M. "Understanding Basic Writers." *English Journal* (Dec. 1988): 77–78

Farr, Marcia, and Harvey Daniels. *Language Diversity and Writing Instruction.* New York: ERIC and NCTE, 1986

Fish, Stanley. *Is There a Text in This Class? The Authority of Interpretive Communities.* Cambridge, MA: Harvard UP, 1980.

Fordham, Synthia. "Racelessness as a Factor in Black Students' School Success: Pragmatic Strategy or Pyrrhic Victory?" *Harvard Educational Review* 58 (Feb. 1988): 54–84.

Foucault, Michel. *Power/Knowledge: Selected Interviews and Other Writings, 1972–77.* Trans. Colin Gordon et al. Ed. Colin Gordon. New York: Pantheon, 1980.

————. "What Is an Author?" *Language, Countermemory, Practice.* Trans. Donald F. Bouchard and Sherry Simon. Ed. Donald F. Bouchard. Ithaca, NY: Cornell UP, 1977. 113–38.

Fowler, Robert J. "An Analysis of the Composing Process of Three Black Adolescents." *DAI* 40 (1980): 4934A. U of Pittsburgh.

Freire, Paulo. *Pedagogy of the Oppressed.* Trans. Myra Bergman Ramos. New York: Herder and Herder, 1972.

Freire, Paulo, and Donaldo Macedo. *Literacy: Reading the Word and the World.* South Hadley, MA: Bergin and Garvey, 1987.

Gates, Henry Louis. "The Blackness of Blackness: A Critique of the Sign and the Signifying Monkey." *Black Literature and Literary Theory.* Ed. Henry Louis Gates. New York: Methuen, 1984. 285–321.

Gilbert, Sandra, and Susan Gubar. *The Madwoman in the Attic: The Woman Writer and the Nineteenth-Century Literary Imagination.* New Haven: Yale UP, 1979.

Gilmore, Perry. " 'Gimme Room': School Resistance, Attitude, and Access to Literacy." *Journal of Education* 167.1 (1985): 111–35.

————. "Spelling Mississippi: Recontextualizing a Literacy-Related Speech Event." *Anthropology and Education Quarterly* 14 (Winter 1983): 235–56.

———. "Sub Rosa Literacy: Peers, Play, and Ownership in Literacy." *The Acquisition of Literacy: Ethnographic Perspectives.* Ed. Bambi Schieffelin and Perry Gilmore. Advances in Discourse Processess Ser. 21. Norwood, NJ: Ablex, 1986. 155–68.

Ginsberg, Allen. "America." *Collected Poems 1947–1980.* New York: Harper & Row, 1982. 146–48.

Goldblatt, Eli. "Kareem Writes About His Neighborhood." Penn State Conference on Rhetoric and Composition, 1991.

Halliday, M.A.K. *Language as Social Semiotic.* London: Edward Arnold, 1978.

Harris, Joseph. "The Idea of Community in the Study of Writing." *College English* 40.1 (Feb. 1989): 11–22.

Hashimoto, I. "Voice as Juice: Some Reservations About Evangelical Composition." *College Composition and Communication* 38.1 (1987): 70–80.

Hatlen, B. "Michel Foucault and the Discourse(s) of English." *College English* 50.7 (1988): 786–801.

Heath, Shirley Brice. *Ways with Words: Language, Life and Work in Communities and Classrooms.* Cambridge: Cambridge UP, 1983.

Hirsch, E. D. *Cultural Literacy.* New York: Vintage, 1988.

Holquist, Michael. "The Politics of Representation." *Allegory and Representation.* Ed. Stephen J. Greenblatt. Baltimore: Johns Hopkins UP, 1982. 163–83.

Holzman, Michael. "The Social Context of Literacy Education." *College English* 48.1 (1986): 27–33.

Horning, Alice S. *Teaching Writing as a Second Language.* Studies in Writing and Rhetoric. Carbondale, IL: Southern Illinois UP, 1987.

Hull, Glynda, Mike Rose, et al. "Remediation as Social Construct: Perspectives from an Analysis of Classroom Discourse." *College Composition and Communication* 42.3 (Oct. 1991): 299–329.

Iser, Wolfgang. *The Act of Reading: A Theory of Aesthetic Response.* Baltimore: Johns Hopkins UP, 1978.

Junker, Clara. "Writing (with) Cixous." *College English* 50.4 (1988): 424–53.

Kiniry, Malcolm, and Mike Rose. *Critical Strategies for Academic Writing.* Boston: Bedford Books, 1990.

Kohl, Herbert. "The Teacher as Learner." *Nation* 16 Apr. 1990: 531–34.

Labov, William. *Language and the Inner City: Studies in the Black English Vernacular.* Philadelphia: U of Pennsylvania P, 1972.

———. "The Study of Language in Its Social Context." *Language and Social Context.* Ed. P. P. Giglioli. Harmondsworth, Eng.: Penguin, 1972. 283–307.

Langer, Judith, and Arthur Applebee. *How Writing Shapes Thinking.* Urbana: NCTE, 1987.

LeFevre, Karen B. *Invention as a Social Act.* Carbondale, IL: Southern Illinois UP, 1987.

Leonardi, Susan J. "Recipes for Reading: Summer Pasta, Lobster á la Rise-holme, and Key Lime Pie." *PMLA* 104.3 (1989): 340–47.

Lunsford, Andrea A. "Assignments for Basic Writers: Unresolved Issues and Needed Research." *Journal of Basic Writing* 5.1 (1986): 87–99.

Lyon, Arabella. "Interdisciplinarity: Giving Up Territory." *College English* 54.6 (Oct. 1992): 681–93.

McGuire, B. S. "Self-Awareness: Toward Greater Control for Young Writers." *English Journal* 77 (1988): 34–36.

Mann, Fred. "Local Angle." *Philadelphia Inquirer Sunday Magazine*. 27 Aug. 1989: 1.

Moffett, James. "Liberating Inner Speech." *College Composition and Communication* 36.3 (1985): 305–08.

———. *Teaching the Universe of Discourse*. 1968. Portsmouth, NH: Boynton/Cook-Heineman, 1983.

Moll, Luis. "Some Key Issues in Teaching Latino Students." *Language Arts* 65.5 (1988): 465–72.

Morison, Samuel Eliot. *The Oxford History of the American People*. New York: Oxford UP, 1965.

Morrow, D. H. "Black American English Style Shifting and Writing Error." *Research in the Teaching of English* 22 (Oct. 1988): 326–40.

———. "Dialect Interference in Writing: Another Critical View." *Research in the Teaching of English* 19 (May 1985): 154–82.

Mortensen, Peter. "Reading Authority, Writing Authority." *Reader* 21 (Spring 1989): 35–55.

Mortensen, Peter, and Gesa E. Kirsch. "On Authority in the Study of Writing." *College Composition and Communication* 44.4 (Dec. 1993): 556–72.

North, Stephen M. *The Making of Knowledge in Composition: Portrait of an Emerging Field*. Upper Montclair, NJ: Boynton/Cook, 1987.

Nystrand, Martin. *The Structure of Written Communication: Studies in Reciprocity Between Writers and Readers*. Orlando: Academic P, 1986.

———. *What Writers Know: The Language, Process, and Structure of Written Discourse*. Orlando: Academic P, 1982.

Odell, Lee. "Beyond the Text: Relations Between Writing and Social Context." *Writing in Nonacademic Settings*. Ed. Lee Odell and Dixie Goswami. New York: Guildford P, 1986. 249–80.

Ogbu, John U. "Cultural-Ecological Influences on Minority School Learning." *Language Arts* 62.8 (1985): 860–69.

———. *The Next Generation: An Ethnography of Education in an Urban Neighborhood*. New York: Academic P, 1974.

Pratt, Mary Louise. "Fieldwork in Common Places." *Writing Culture: The Poetics and Politics of Ethnography*. Ed. James Clifford and George E. Marcus. Berkeley: U of California P, 1986. 27–50.

———. *Imperial Eyes: Travel Writing and Transculturation.* London and New York: Routledge, 1992.

———. "Linguistic Utopias." *The Linguistics of Writing.* Manchester, Gt. Brit.: Manchester UP, 1987. 48–66.

Rodriguez, Richard. *Hunger of Memory.* Boston: David Godine, 1982.

Rommetveit, R. *On Message Structure: A Framework for the Study of Language and Communication.* London: Wiley and Sons, 1974.

Rose, Mike. *Lives on the Boundary: The Struggles and Achievements of America's Underprepared.* New York: Free Press-Macmillan, 1989.

Said, Edward W. "Opponents, Audiences, Constituencies and Community." *Critical Inquiry* 9 (Sept. 1982): 1–26.

Shaughnessy, Mina. *Errors and Expectations.* New York: Oxford UP, 1977.

Shor, Ira, and Paulo Freire. *A Pedagogy for Liberation: Dialogues on Transforming Education.* South Hadley, MA: Bergin and Garvey, 1987.

Sledd, Andrew. "Reading not Riotin': The Politics of Literacy." *College English* 50.5 (1988): 495–508.

Sledd, James. "Bidialectalism: The Linguistics of White Supremacy." *English Journal* 58.9 (1969): 1307–15.

Smith, David. "The Anthropology of Literacy Acquisition." *The Acquisition of Literacy: Ethnographic Perspectives.* Advances in Discourse Processess Ser. 21. Ed. Bambi Schieffelin and Perry Gilmore. Norwood, NJ: Ablex, 1986. 261–75.

Smitherman, Geneva. "English Teacher, Why You Be Doing the Thangs You Don't Do?" *English Journal* 61 (Jan. 1972): 59–65.

———. *Talkin' and Testifyin': The Language of Black America.* Boston: Houghton Mifflin, 1977.

So, A. Y. "High Achieving Disadvantaged Students: A Study of Low SES Hispanic Language Minority Youth." *Urban Education* 22 (Apr. 1987): 19–35.

Sola, Michele, and Adrian T. Bennett. "The Struggle for Voice: Narrative, Literacy and Consciousness in an East Harlem School." *Journal of Education* 167.1 (1985): 88–110.

Sternglass, Marilyn S. "Dialect Features in the Composition of Black and White College Students: The Same or Different?" *College Composition and Communication* 25.3 (1974): 259–63.

"Students' Right to Their Own Language." *College Composition and Communication* 25.3 (1974): 1–32.

Taylor, Denny, and Catherine Dorsey-Gaines. *Growing Up Literate: Learning from Inner-City Families.* Portsmouth, NH: Heinemann, 1988.

Tuman, Myron C. "Class, Codes, and Composition: Basil Bernstein and the Critique of Pedagogy." *College Composition and Communication* 39.1 (1988): 42–51.

Valverde, Sylvia A. "A Comparative Study of Hispanic High School Dropouts
and Graduates: Why Do Some Leave School Early and Some Finish?"
Education and Urban Society 19.3 (1987): 320–29.

Wigginton, Eliot. *Sometimes a Shining Moment: The Foxfire Experiment.* New
York: Anchor-Doubleday, 1986.

Williams, Patricia. *The Alchemy of Race and Rights.* Cambridge, MA: Harvard
UP, 1991.

Williams, Silvia B. "A Comparative Study of Black Dropouts and Black High
School Graduates in an Urban Public School System." *Education and
Urban Society* 19.3 (1987): 311–19.

About the Author

Eli Goldblatt was born in 1952 in Cleveland, Ohio, and grew up on Army posts in the United States and Germany. After college and odd jobs in farming, manufacture, and carpentry, as well as a year in medical school, he taught science and math for six years in an inner-city alternative high school in Philadelphia. He studied literature and composition at the University of Wisconsin-Madison, and is currently an assistant professor of English at Villanova University.

He has previously published two children's books (*Leo Loves Round* and *Lissa and the Moon's Sheep*, Harbinger House), one verse play (*Herakles*, Tamarask Press), and two books of poetry: *Journeyman's Song* (Coffeehouse Press) and *Sessions 1–62* (Chax Press). He lives in Philadelphia with his wife, visual artist Wendy Osterweil, and their son Leo.

Pittsburgh Series in Composition, Literacy, and Culture

David Bartholomae and Jean Ferguson Carr, Editors

Academic Discourse and Critical Consciousness
Patricia Bizzell

Between Languages and Cultures: Translation and Cross-cultural Texts
Anuradha Dingwaney and Carol Maier, Editors

Eating on the Street: Teaching Literacy in a Multicultural Society
David Schaafsma

The Emperor's New Clothes: Literature, Literacy,
and the Ideology of Style
Kathryn T. Flannery

Feminine Principles and Women's Experience in American
Composition and Rhetoric
Louise Wetherbee Phelps and Janet Emig, Editors

Fragments of Rationality: Postmodernity and the Subject of Composition
Lester Faigley

The Insistence of the Letter: Literacy Studies and Curriculum Theories
Bill Green, Editor

Knowledge, Culture, and Power: International Perspectives
on Literacy as Policy and Practice
Peter Freebody and Anthony R. Welch, Editors

The Labyrinths of Literacy: Reflections on Literacy Past and Present
Harvey J. Graff

Literacy Online: The Promise (and Peril) of Reading
and Writing with Computers
Myron C. Tuman, Editor

The Origins of Composition Studies in the American College
1875–1925: A Documentary History
John C. Brereton, Editor

The Powers of Literacy: A Genre Approach to Teaching Writing
Bill Cope and Mary Kalantzis, Editors

Pre/Text: The First Decade
Victor Vitanza, Editor

Reclaiming Rhetorica: Women in the Rhetorical Tradition
Andrea A. Lunsford, Editor

'Round My Way: Authority and Double-Consciousness in Three
Urban High School Writers
Eli C. Goldblatt

Word Perfect: Literacy in the Computer Age
Myron C. Tuman

Writing Science: Literacy and Discursive Power
M.A.K. Halliday and J. R. Martin